Smart Guide™
to
Managing Personal Finance

About Smart Guides™

Welcome to Smart Guides. Each Smart Guide is created as a written conversation with a learned friend; a skilled and knowledgeable author guides you through the basics of the subject, selecting out the most important points and skipping over anything that's not essential. Along the way, you'll also find smart inside tips and strategies that distinguish this from other books on the topic.

Within each chapter you'll find a number of recurring features to help you find your way through the information and put it to work for you. Here are the user-friendly elements you'll encounter and what they mean:

The Keys
Each chapter opens by highlighting in overview style the most important concepts in the pages that follow.

Smart Money
Here's where you will learn opinions and recommendations from experts and professionals in the field.

Street Smarts
This feature presents smart ways in which people have dealt with related issues and shares their secrets for success.

Smart Sources
Each of these sidebars points the way to more and authoritative information on the topic, from organizations, corporations, publications, web sites, and more.

Smart Definition
Terminology and key concepts essential to your mastering the subject matter are clearly explained in this feature.

F.Y.I.
Related facts, statistics, and quick points of interest are noted here.

The Bottom Line
The conclusion to each chapter, here is where the lessons learned in each section are summarized so you can revisit the most essential information of the text.

One of the main objectives of the *Smart Guide to Managing Personal Finance* is not only to better inform you about important financial concerns, but to make you smarter about money and investments to ensure a lifetime of security for yourself and your family.

Smart Guide™

to

Managing Personal Finance

Alfred and Emily Glossbrenner

CADER BOOKS

John Wiley & Sons, Inc.

New York • Chichester • Weinheim • Brisbane • Singapore • Toronto

Library of Congress Cataloging-in-Publication Data:
Glossbrenner, Alfred.
Smart guide to managing personal finance / Alfred and Emily
Glossbrenner.
p.   cm.   — (Smart guide)
Includes index.
ISBN 0-471-29604-X
1. Finance, Personal. I. Glossbrenner, Emily. II. Title.
III. Series.
HG179.G554   1998
332.024—dc21   98-34844

Printed in the United States of America

10 9 8 7 6 5 4 3 2 1

Contents

Introduction

We all know that money truly is one of the essences of real life. Art, music, culture, family, travel, recreation, and sports—there isn't anything you can name that could not be improved and enhanced by your having more money. And that is really what this book is all about.

Personal finance is not a given. It doesn't happen automatically. And, with all due respect, sitting down with your paycheck once or twice a month and deciding which bills you can pay is no way to prosper and get ahead. Regardless of how much you earn, you need to take control. You need to say, "Okay, enough! I'm not going to spend the rest of my life living from paycheck to paycheck." That's why this book begins with a chapter on taking control of your personal finances.

Once you're onboard, you'll need a bank, so the next chapter tells you what to look for and what to avoid. Credit cards and credit reports, buying or leasing a car, and buying a home or condo are covered in the following chapters. The insights and insiders' tips and tricks you'll encounter here could save you hundreds, even thousands, of dollars.

But simply acquiring a home or a car or anything else isn't enough. Not in today's world. How do you shield yourself and your family from loss? And how do you make sure you're not driven to bankruptcy if you become disabled? And what about making sense of all the various options for health insurance?

Once you've gotten your personal-financial

house in order and have made certain that your loved ones are protected, it may be time to think about investing. You may find that chapter to be one of the most eye-opening of all. In fact, if you're already an active investor, you may want to read it first.

The book concludes with chapters devoted to saving for college and retirement, coping with taxes, and estate planning. These may well be the most important chapters in the book. Why? Because they will alert you to strategies you can use to boost the amount of financial aid you can get for college, reduce the amount of taxes you pay, and make sure that as much as possible of your estate goes to your heirs instead of to the government.

Some personal-finance books skim the surface and offer little more than eye-candy graphics. Others delve so deep that you soon find yourself awash in information, much of which doesn't apply to your situation. The goal of the *Smart Guide to Managing Personal Finance* is to suggest ways of thinking about money and investments, and to offer sound advice on the steps you should take when you have a concern.

Each chapter ends with a short section called "The Bottom Line." The bottom line for the book as a whole is simple: Money is important, and the way you handle it makes a difference—for you and for those you love. But money doesn't manage itself. *You* must take charge. The chapters in this book can be an enormous help in showing you what you need to do as you explore the ins and outs of being smart about personal finance. They will point you in the right direction.

Go ahead. Take that first step!

Taking Control of Your Personal Finances

Everyone likes to spend money. But few of us like to spend the time and effort needed to get—and keep—our personal finances in order, even though doing so would almost certainly help us have more money to spend. Often, a lot more.

Contrary to what you may think, managing your personal finances isn't hard. What's hard is getting yourself to do what needs to be done, a task complicated by the fact that most people haven't a clue about what that might be.

In this chapter, you'll learn exactly what to do to get smart about managing your finances. You'll eliminate the need to hire a financial planner, who'd probably charge you anywhere from $200 to $2,500 to do the work for you. And you'll discover that getting smart about your personal finances can actually be a lot of fun, to say nothing of the satisfaction of feeling that (finally!) you're in control.

What Are You Worth?

Start by figuring your net worth. In banker's terms, net worth is the sum of your financial assets minus the sum of your financial liabilities. To put it more simply, it's the number you arrive at when you subtract the dollar value of what you owe from the dollar value of what you own.

Figuring your net worth the first time will take some time. The worksheet provided in this chapter will be a big help, but you'll still have to assemble the information. Be sure to do this in a way that makes it easy to repeat the process a year from now. A box of manila folders and a filing cabinet (or a heavy-duty plastic or cardboard storage box from your local office-supply store) will help you get things organized. Computer programs like Quicken, Microsoft Money, and Managing Your Money have built-in forms for net-worth calculations, making it easy to perform the arithmetic and to keep your worksheets up to date.

Why Should You Care?

Figuring your net worth is work. So take your time, and take it easy. Try to have fun with it. After all, you're counting up your money! And that can be a pleasurable process.

It's also an important process. Knowing your net worth allows you to drive a stake in the ground and say, "Okay, this is where I am." Only after doing that can you then say, "Now, where do I want to go?" A year from now, you should calculate your net worth again to measure the progress you've made. The idea is to see your net worth steadily increase year after year.

You'll also be prepared and ready for those financial situations that call for information about your current net worth. When you apply for a mortgage or line of credit, fill out college financial-aid forms, increase your life insurance coverage, or sign up for an investment opportunity with a minimum-net-worth requirement, you'll be glad you've done your homework.

STREET SMARTS

"I used to wake up in a cold sweat," says Sean, owner of a small tree-service company. "Business is good, and my wife, Joan, works part-time. But the money just goes!

"We tried a so-called financial planner, but he turned out to be just another insurance salesman in disguise. We contacted a mutual fund firm that said it would prepare a plan for $500. But the only funds it would recommend were its own.

"Then one of my buddies and I were having a beer and he said, 'Why don't you do your own financial plan? I mean it's not like it's brain surgery. It's not even tree surgery.'

"So I got some books and looked at the money-oriented magazines at the library. And you know what? You really can do it yourself. You simply have to do it!"

SMART SOURCES

Here are the leading personal-finance software programs:

Quicken
Quicken Basic 98 ($40) does checking, online banking, budgeting, and investment tracking. Quicken Home & Business 98 ($90) has features for small businesses.
800-446-8848
www.quicken.com

Microsoft Money
Money 98 is $30. For $55, the Money 98 Financial Suite provides an Advisor FYI module to analyze and make suggestions, Goal Planner, and automatic monthly reports.
800-426-9400
www.moneyinsider.msn.com

Managing Your Money
Created by financial writer Andrew Tobias, MYM ($30) is particularly strong in producing reports, projections, and graphs.
203-452-2600
www.mymnet.com

How to Figure Your Net Worth

Use any system you like—the Net Worth Worksheet provided here, personal-finance software if you have it, or simply paper and pencil. You'll find it to be an eye-opening exercise, particularly if you're thirty- or forty-something and have been working steadily since graduating from high school or college. For example, the assets in your checking and savings accounts are obvious. But what's the value of your 401(k) retirement plan? Your IRA or Keogh account? What about your pension, if you have one, or any stock options you may be fortunate enough to own?

Adding Up Your Assets

Fill in the easy stuff first—the balances in your checking and savings accounts and the latest numbers reported on your 401(k), IRA, and Keogh statements. Then move on to assets like your house, cars, boats, a second home, other real-estate holdings, and so on. What's their *fair market* value? In other words, what could you sell them for today? You'll also need to go from room to room in your house and create a list of personal possessions that are especially valuable—furniture, jewelry, antiques, collections, and so forth.

You don't have to be precise, but you have to be realistic. That bejeweled Victorian hat pin that once belonged to your great-grandmother may look like it cost a fortune, but it might not be worth what you think. On the other hand, that rather odd-looking oak chair that you long ago relegated to the basement could be a genuine antique worth thousands of dollars.

Does anyone owe you any money, either to pay back a loan or for goods and services provided? Take this into account. But don't include future salary payments. You're developing a snapshot of your net worth right now, so payment for hours not yet spent on the job shouldn't be included.

Adding Up Your Liabilities

Of course, there's also the other side of the equation: what you owe. This is not the amount you pay to various creditors each month. Rather, it's your total debt. For example, in calculating your assets, you estimated what you could get for your house if you sold it today. On your liabilities list, you need to write down the outstanding balance on your mortgage, since that balance would have to be paid off if you did sell your home.

Total credit-card debt. Home-equity loan payments. Student loans. Income and real-estate taxes that are due. Identifying your liabilities is rarely as challenging as identifying your assets. That's because creditors typically make a point of making themselves known to you.

Don't get tangled up in ongoing monthly expenses like rent or utilities. You're not counting future paychecks among your assets, so there is no sense counting future monthly bills for commodities not yet delivered or consumed. The watchword is "What would I have left if I were to liquidate all my assets and pay off all my debts today?"

SMART DEFINITION

Fair Market Value
The price that a knowledgeable, rational, and willing buyer would pay for the things you want to sell.

Net Worth Worksheet

Assets

Checking Accounts
& Cash . . . . _____

Savings Accounts . . . . _____

IRA & Keogh
Accounts . . . . _____

Stocks & Bonds . . . . _____

Mutual Funds . . . . _____

Pension &
401(k) Plans . . . . _____

Life Insurance
Cash Value . . . . _____

Real Estate

   Home . . . . _____

   Other Real Estate . . . . . . _____

Personal Property
(cars, furniture, jewelry,
silver, furs, boats, tools,
collectibles) . . . . _____

Amounts Owed to Me
(loans and money due
for work already
performed) . . . . _____

Equity Value of
a Business . . . . _____

Other Assets

_____ . . . . _____

_____ . . . . _____

_____ . . . . _____

Total Assets . . . . _____

Liabilities

Mortgages . . . . _____

Home-Equity Loans . . . . . _____

Car Loans . . . . _____

Credit-Card Debt . . . . _____

Personal Loans . . . . _____

Student Loans . . . . _____

Other Loans . . . . _____

Taxes Owed

   Income . . . . _____

   Real Estate . . . . _____

Other Liabilities

_____ . . . . _____

_____ . . . . _____

_____ . . . . _____

Total Liabilities . . . . . . _____

Net Worth (Assets minus Liabilities) [   ]

How Does Your Net Worth Stack Up?

Once you've figured your net worth, you can use the information presented here to get a rough idea of how your financial situation compares to that of other U.S. families in your age group. The numbers are based on 1995 data and thus don't take into consideration the run-up of the stock market in recent years.

Age (Head of Household)	Average Net Worth
Under 35	$47,200
35-44	$144,500
45-54	$277,800
55-64	$356,200
65-74	$331,600
75+	$276,000

Source: Federal Reserve System

Where Would You Like to Go?

Now for the fun part. Now you get to identify and clarify your financial dreams and goals. So sit back and think about the future you'd like to have. For example, everyone wants a comfortable retirement, but maybe what you'd really like is a com-

SMART MONEY

There are at least two side benefits to the process of getting a handle on your assets. First, your review of the real estate and personal property you own will make it much easier to determine how much home-owner's insurance you should buy. Second, the exercise of figuring your net worth forces you to organize most of your important house-hold and financial records. Once you've done that, it's an easy next step to make sure that they're stored in a safe place. One option is to put them in a safe-deposit box at your bank. But you may find it cheaper and more convenient to spend $130 or so on a fire safe. Fire safes usually have combination locks for security, but their primary purpose is to safe-guard vital documents against fire, not against theft by a burglar.

fortable early retirement. Or maybe you want to retire at sixty-five but also have enough extra money to do a lot of traveling.

Saving for retirement, building a nest egg, creating an estate for your heirs—these are all long-range goals. Medium-range dreams might include buying a vacation home in several years or taking a trip around the world; saving to have a baby or to send a child to college are other good examples. Short-term goals are those you hope to accomplish in the next year or two, such as paying down your credit-card debt or buying a car.

And then there are the goals that are less enjoyable to think about—making sure you have enough insurance, for example, or building up an emergency fund to carry you for three to six months should you become the victim of downsizing or meet with some other misfortune. In fact, you might be concerned that once you've done all the sensible, prudent things, there won't be enough money left for the fun things.

That doesn't have to be the case, any more than you have to do without adequate insurance coverage or savings because you want to take the family to Disney World. You may not be able to go to Disney World right now, or even next year, but if you're smart about it, and if you plan, you can do it at some point. So take a moment to actually write down your goals and your dreams. Then move to the next step—planning.

Planning Your Spending and Saving

The traditional way to plot a path to your financial goals is to create a budget and then live by it. But as one of today's teenagers might say, "Get real!" Certainly there are people who can successfully stick to a strict budget. But most of us can't, just as most of us can't completely give up ice cream or some other indulgence for an extended period of time.

The key word here is *completely*. Perhaps instead of having ice cream for dessert every night, you eat a piece of fresh fruit for one or two nights of the week. Or instead of sliding from dessert straight into an evening of television, you take a walk around the block after dinner and then watch TV. These are small lifestyle changes that you will hardly feel, but over time they can have a major positive impact on your health.

The same is true of your "money lifestyle" and your financial health. A few small adjustments can pay truly huge financial dividends. To make those adjustments, you need to get a handle on your current spending ("Where does the money go?"). Then you need to get smart about cutting expenses and channeling the money saved into investments. After all, regardless of your specific dreams and goals, everything begins with accumulating and investing the amount of money that will enable you to meet those dreams and goals.

Does that mean that you're going to have to do without? Not necessarily. It might simply mean that you'll have to do without right now. As *Newsweek* columnist and financial expert Jane Bryant Quinn says, "Good financial planning starts from where you are and makes things better."

Can You Find $5 a Day?

The question is this: Can you reduce your current spending by $5 a day, seven days a week, for a total savings of $35 a week? For the high rollers of the world, that might mean having espresso for dessert at lunch instead of the crème brûlée. For others, it might mean brown-bagging it three days a week instead of going out. For still others, it might mean buying a less expensive but perfectly acceptable bottle of wine to have with dinner at home. There are lots of ways to cut costs without eliminating pleasures.

Basically, almost anyone can find a way to cut expenses by $5 a day. That adds up to about $150 a month or $1,800 a year. Not chump change, but not something to get excited about, either. Or is it?

Let's assume you're thirty-five years old and have another thirty years to work before retiring. If you can put $1,800 this year into a tax-deferred retirement account earning an average annual return of 10 percent, by the time you turn sixty-five that $1,800 will have grown to nearly $30,000. All from cutting your expenses by an average of $5 a day for just one year. If you were to do this when you were twenty-nine, your single investment of $1,800 will have grown to nearly $60,000 by the time you're sixty-five.

Put It on Paper

The first step is to make a list of everything you spend money on in the course of a month. For big, once-a-year items like vacations, lump-sum property taxes, or major purchases made during the year, divide the amount by 12.

Start with your taxes. Then do house-related expenses such as your mortgage or rent, phone, cable TV, water, gas, electricity, maintenance, and repairs. Next, focus on clothing and food. And don't forget snacks and the coffee and bagel you buy on the train or at the office each morning.

Now that you're housed, clothed, and fed, think about recreation: movies (including the popcorn and soda), video rentals, books, magazines, newspapers, hobbies, pets, etc.

Use the suggested expense categories in the Spending Worksheet we've provided to get started. Then consult your checkbook and credit-card statements. And don't be too quick to complete this little exercise. In fact, you might want to return to your list several times during a typical week to record items that you missed.

The Expense- Reduction Game

Once you've got your list of expenses, consider each one and ask yourself if there is a way to reduce it. This will take some time, but you'll be well paid for your efforts. And it really is true that getting smart about reducing expenses can be an enjoyable game. As you play it, however, don't assume you cannot cut an expense until you've really pushed things to the limit.

For example, you might think that the only way to reduce your electric bill is to be more vigilant about turning off lights in unoccupied rooms. But depending on where you live, if you have an electric water heater, you can probably save $300

SMART MONEY

The startling numbers in our retirement example come from applying the famous Rule of 72. For mathematical reasons that need not concern us, the Rule of 72 will tell you how soon your money will double at a given rate of interest. Just divide 72 by the interest rate your investment is earning. Thus, if your money is earning 10 percent, it will double in 7.2 years. At 15 percent, it will double in 4.8 years.

This assumes that interest is not taxed, and it makes no allowance for inflation. Nor has the difference between investing pre-tax and after-tax dollars been considered here. The main message is this: Investing as little as $1,800 a year ($5 a day) in a tax-deferred account won't inconvenience you much at all, but it can lead to a big payoff when you retire.

or more each year by having the electric company install an off-peak meter. (The savings come from the lower electric rate charged for running the water heater during off-peak hours.) You can save another $75 a year if you agree to have your electric dryer hooked up to the meter as well. And $75 more if you add your clothes washer.

And what about all those brand-name products you buy each week at the grocery store? *Consumer Reports* frequently compares food, paper, and cleaning products and finds little or no difference between generic (or store-brand) and brand-name items. If you're determined to stick with your favorite brands, make a habit of shopping at warehouse stores like Sam's Club or PriceCostco, where you can find them at 30 to 40 percent discounts. If your family of four spends an average of $280 a week on food and drugstore items, figuring low, you can easily save $35 a week by buying in bulk (12 roles of Bounty paper towels per package instead of three, for example). And, assuming storage isn't a problem, you may even find that it's more convenient to shop this way, since it reduces the number of times you have to go to the store. Once you get into the swing of things, you're sure to come up with simple, easy, and, above all, *painless* ways to cut your expenses.

Taking Action: Are Your Expenses in the Zone?

Another important aspect of your spending analysis is comparing your new spending plan with your total income. There are two possible approaches to doing this. You can add up an entire year's expenses and income, or you can focus on a typical month. If you opt for the monthly approach, just be sure that you've captured extraordinary expenses such as vacations, major car maintenance, furniture purchases, annual insurance premiums, and so on. Simply add them up, divide by 12, and apply the result to your list of a typical month's expenses.

Then take a look at some of the bigger items and see how they compare to your overall income. As a general rule of thumb, for example, most financial experts recommend that you spend no more than 30 percent of your take-home (or after-tax) pay on mortgage or rent. You should try to save between 10 and 20 percent of your paycheck. (Though it may be hard to reach, putting 10 percent into a tax-deferred retirement plan and another 5 percent into other kinds of nonretirement savings is a good goal.) Finally, your total debt, not including your mortgage, should be less than 20 percent of your annual take-home pay. (Get your total debt figure from your Net Worth Worksheet.)

If, in your best estimate, your expenses exceed your income, you will simply have to find a way to cut expenses further. That could pinch. The emphasis thus far has been on cutting expenses by being smarter, without sacrificing lifestyle. But if your income and expenses are seriously out of whack, you have no choice but to find further reductions—even if that means moving to a less expensive home or selling your second car. Alternatively, to look on the positive side, you can try to boost your income by getting a second job, asking your current employer for a raise, or finding a new job at a higher rate of pay.

The equations are remorseless. You may be able to slide by for a while, but if your expenses

Spending Worksheet

Expense Categories	Current Monthly Spending($)	Possible Cuts($)	Expense Categories	Current Monthly Spending($)	Possible Cuts($)
Taxes			Furniture & Appliances	_____	_____
Federal Income Tax	_____	_____	Maintenance & Repairs	_____	_____
Social Security & Medicare	_____	_____	*Food and Drink*		
State & Local Taxes	_____	_____	Groceries	_____	_____
			Restaurant Meals	_____	_____
Housing			Takeout	_____	_____
Mortgage or Rent	_____	_____	Beer, Wine, & Liquor	_____	_____
Property Taxes	_____	_____			
Gas, Electric, Heating Oil	_____	_____	*Clothes and Shoes*		
Telephone	_____	_____	Family Member 1:	_____	_____
Cable TV	_____	_____	Family Member 2:	_____	_____
Water & Sewer	_____	_____	Family Member 3:	_____	_____
Trash Collection	_____	_____	Family Member 4:	_____	_____
Cleaning Service & Supplies	_____	_____	Dry Cleaning	_____	_____
Lawn Service	_____	_____	Shoe Repair	_____	_____

Expense Categories	Current Monthly Spending($)	Possible Cuts($)	Expense Categories	Current Monthly Spending($)	Possible Cuts($)
Transportation			Cosmetics & Toiletries	_____	_____
Gasoline & Motor Oil	_____	_____	Health Club Membership	_____	_____
Car Maintenance & Repairs	_____	_____	**Health Care**		
Tolls & Parking Fees	_____	_____	Doctor Visits	_____	_____
Public Transportation	_____	_____	Prescription Drugs	_____	_____
			Dental Care	_____	_____
Recreation			Eye Care, Glasses, & Contacts	_____	_____
Books, Magazines, & Newspapers	_____	_____	Medical Supplies	_____	_____
Movies, Concerts, & Plays	_____	_____	**Insurance**		
Sports Events	_____	_____	Homeowner's/ Renter's	_____	_____
Online Services	_____	_____	Auto	_____	_____
Hobbies	_____	_____	Life	_____	_____
Pets & Pet Care	_____	_____	Health	_____	_____
Video/Audio Rentals	_____	_____	Disability	_____	_____
			Flood	_____	_____
Vacations & Travel	_____	_____	Earthquake	_____	_____
Personal Care			**Education**		
Haircuts	_____	_____	Tuition & Fees	_____	_____

Spending Worksheet continued on page 16

Expense Categories	Current Monthly Spending($)	Possible Cuts($)	Expense Categories	Current Monthly Spending($)	Possible Cuts($)
Books & Supplies	_____	_____	*Other Expenses* Accountant	_____	_____
Children Day Care & Baby-sitters	_____	_____	Bank Charges & Fees	_____	_____
Toys & Playground Equipment	_____	_____	Charitable Contributions	_____	_____
After-School Activities	_____	_____	Club Memberships	_____	_____
Debt Repayments Credit Cards	_____	_____	Credit-Card Memberships	_____	_____
Car Loans	_____	_____	Gifts (Birthday, Holiday, etc.)	_____	_____
Home-Equity Loans	_____	_____	Legal Fees	_____	_____
Student Loans	_____	_____	Other	_____	_____
			Other	_____	_____
			Other	_____	_____
			Spending Totals	_____	_____

always exceed your income and you don't do something, you will indeed go bankrupt. Should that happen, your creditors may take the decision out of your hands and sell your house and possessions to pay your debts.

Monthly Cash Flow

Monthly Income

Salary (before tax) . . . . _____

Overtime Pay (before tax) . . . . _____

Bonuses & Commissions (before tax) . . . . _____

Investment Income (interest & dividends) . . . . _____

Other Income . . . . _____

Total Monthly Income . . . . _____

Monthly Expenses (from Spending Worksheet) . . . . -_____

Monthly Surplus or Shortfall . . . . _____

Paying Down Your Credit Cards

You may have heard it said that 90 percent of success in life is the result of just showing up. Although we don't have statistics to support the idea, it's probably fair to say that 90 percent of financial and investment success is just taking the time to pay attention. Stop for a moment or two in your daily routine and take the time to really examine your finances. The current and future benefits can be enormous.

Nowhere is this more true than when considering credit-card debt. According to the Consumer Federation of America, the average credit-card debt for U.S. households is $7,000. And each of an

SMART SOURCES

Contrary to popular belief, creditors take no pleasure in putting people out on the street. They'll work with you if you're in trouble, because it's in their best interest to do so. But you have to take the first step. Here are some good credit counseling services for a start:

Credit Counseling Centers of America
800-493-2222
www.cccamerica.org

Debtors Anonymous
212-642-8220 (call for referral to groups in your area)
www.debtorsanonymous. org

National Foundation for Consumer Credit
800-388-2227
www.nfcc.org

estimated 55 to 60 million households pays an average of $1,000 a year in interest and fees. It's no wonder that Opinion Research Corporation reports that 36 percent of all households are "very concerned" about meeting their monthly bills.

Clearly, the first step for many of us should be to dramatically reduce credit-card debt and interest payments. Easier said than done, of course. But think about it. You've probably used your credit cards to buy furniture, appliances, electronics equipment, and a lot of other great stuff. How much more do you need? Couldn't you cut up one or more of your credit cards and work out a plan for paying them off? Some experts recommend borrowing against your retirement plan or using a home-equity loan to pay off credit cards. But this strategy only works if you can permanently break the credit-card habit, something that not many of us can do.

Still, consider the benefits. If you were to take that $1,000 you may be paying each year in annual credit-card interest and fees ($83 a month) and invest it at 10 percent, tax-deferred, for thirty years, it would grow to nearly $190,000. If you're paying $2,000 a year ($167 a month) in interest and fees and you could invest that amount instead, you would have $380,000 after thirty years. (Personal finance software programs like Quicken, Microsoft Money, and Managing Your Own Money include "What-if?" calculators that make it easy to do this type of interest-rate and investment analysis.)

Internalizing the Plan and Goals

Paying off credit-card debt may well be the single

most important and most difficult of all financial goals. It goes without saying that you should leave your cards at home whenever you go shopping and start paying for everything with cash, something that is much easier to do these days, thanks to credit card–like debit cards.

But the first thing you should do is not all that obvious: Commit yourself to the goal of paying off your credit-card debt. You have to internalize the goal and really feel it. That way, when you want to blow $75 on dinner out, or you're tempted to spend $45 for a new power tool, *not doing so* will have a purpose. You won't be denying yourself simply to save money. You will be working toward a goal.

The same approach applies if you have children. Their wants are endless, their needs are not. Deal with their wants by bringing them into the plan and getting their input and their commitment. Have a real sit-down meeting to discuss household finances and goals. If you set as a family goal a visit to Disney World, for example, your daughter may still ask for those $150 in-line skates, but she's more likely to understand when you say no or have to postpone the purchase. Kids are smart. They'll try for all they can get, but they will understand if you treat them like adults and bring them fully into the goal-setting process.

Finding Ways to Pay Off Your Credit Cards

Let's assume that you owe the national average of $7,000 on your credit cards and that you're paying 18 percent interest. To eliminate that debt in a single year, you'd have to make payments of $642

SMART DEFINITION

Debit cards
They look just like credit cards, but they work like checks. When you use a debit card, the amount of the purchase is withdrawn from your checking account, so there's no interest to pay or end-of-the-month bill to contend with.

a month, which may well be impossible. But maybe you can do it in two years with payments of $350 a month, or in three years ($253 a month), or even four years ($206 a month).

After all, it probably took you a couple of years or more to run up that much debt, so it will naturally take some time to pay it off. Whatever you do, don't neglect such crucial safety-net features as life, home, car, and liability insurance, even if it means that paying off your credit cards will take longer. Consider these ideas instead:

• The next time you get a raise, apply the extra money in each month's paycheck to your credit-card debt. Don't simply begin to spend more. Do the same with any bonuses or overtime payments you receive until the credit cards are paid off.

• Cut back on holiday and birthday gift-giving, and encourage your friends and relatives to do the same. (They'll very likely welcome the idea.) Be creative. Instead of buying gifts for everyone on your list, consider setting up a "Pollyanna" gift exchange, with each person drawing a name at random and shopping for (or making) a single gift.

• Postpone major home-maintenance expenses. Make temporary repairs yourself, if necessary, but hold off on the big stuff. Sure, the house would look better with a fresh coat of paint, but if it's simply a question of cosmetics (not protecting your investment), try to make the current paint job last an extra year.

• Readjust your thinking about how you spend your annual vacation. Instead of traveling to some exotic locale, try "vacationing at home"—taking day trips, eating out, doing whatever you feel like doing from morning till night. Apply the money you would have spent on airfare and overnight accommodations to your credit-card debt.

Saving the Savings

With your credit-card debt reduced to zero (or at least under control), make the commitment to save between 10 and 20 percent of your take-home pay. You'll learn more in Chapter 9, but 401(k) plans and their relatives are among the best deals going. They're funded with pre-tax dollars, and the contributions you make may be matched 25 to 50 percent by your employer. Your money and earnings accumulate untaxed for years and years.

Best of all for someone trying to keep debt under control, you never see the money because it is automatically deducted from your paycheck. Automatic deductions are the surest way to make yourself save, so if your employer doesn't offer a 401(k) plan, see about having money deducted on a monthly basis from your savings or checking account to fund an IRA. Most mutual funds offer an automatic monthly investment option, and you can authorize them to deduct and invest as little as $25 to $50 a month.

THE BOTTOM LINE

In order to take control of your personal finances, you have to get a handle on your net worth and your monthly spending habits. Once you have that information, you can focus on ways to reduce spending so that you'll have more money left at the end of each month to apply to investments and other goals.

The key to achieving nearly any financial dream is really quite simple: Spend less than you earn and invest the rest. It's not easy, but it's simple. Fortunately, doing the right thing does not have to be painful. Think of a boat crossing the ocean. On a long trip, an all-but-imperceptible change in direction of but a few compass points will have a huge effect on where you land at the end of your journey.

CHAPTER 2

....

Shopping for a Bank

Everyone needs a bank—or a credit union or savings and loan association (S&L). At least, everyone with bills to pay and a salary to deposit. Unfortunately, choosing the bank that's right for you is both harder and easier than ever before. It's harder because many banks now have so many different fees and charges for nearly everything. Indeed, the differences among banks are so great that you could find yourself wasting upward of $200 a year if you don't pay attention.

What makes selecting a bank easier is that the personal banker—the longtime branch manager or vice president who knew you and your family—has gone the way of the personal physician who made house calls. For some years, big banks have been buying up smaller banks at a rapid pace. Personal relationships may still matter in small towns, but for most people today, there are just two issues to consider: convenience and cost.

Convenience and Cost

Banks, credit unions, and S&Ls are still good places to go for mortgages and car loans, and it's always a good idea to introduce yourself to the branch manager. But you're likely to use checking accounts and automated teller machines (ATMs) the most, so be sure to ask these questions:

• Where are the bank's branches, drive-through windows, and supermarket outposts?

• Where are the bank's own ATMs, and what does it cost to use them?

• What does it cost to use *another* bank's (or a third party's) ATMs?

• What's it going to cost to maintain and use my checking account?

Where Are the Branches and the ATMs?

Years ago, the really clever city people would open an account with a small-town bank back home or elsewhere, make deposits by mail, and use that account to pay all their bills. Doing so gave them the advantage of lower small-town banking fees, and their checks took perhaps an extra day to clear. Local merchants are never happy to accept out-of-town checks, but landlords, utilities, and credit-card companies rarely complain.

Some people still do this. But banking, like everything else, has changed. Now, according to the Bank Administration Institute of Chicago, 57 percent of consumers use ATMs and 67 percent use drive-through windows—features that are either more expensive or not available if you use an out-of-town bank. With most people using ATMs and drive-throughs, it's not surprising that geographical convenience rather than fees has become the most important consideration when choosing a bank.

Checking Your Checking Habits

To make sense of the many checking-account options banks offer, you will want to ask yourself the following questions:

1. What's your average monthly balance? (If you've never had an account before, try estimating your monthly bills and subtracting the sum from your monthly income.)

2. How many checks do you typically write each month?

3. How many deposits do you make each month?

4. Can your employer automatically deposit your paycheck?

5. How often do you use ATMs each month to withdraw money?

Still, the ATM transaction fees charged when you use machines not "owned" by your bank can eat you alive. If you do most of your banking via ATM, it just makes good sense to start your search with the banks whose own ATMs are most convenient to your home or work locations.

Three Main Kinds of Checking Accounts

Once you've identified the banks with the most convenient branches, drive-throughs, and ATMs, focus on how each bank charges for checking accounts. There are three main kinds of checking accounts:

1. Special or Budget Checking. These are basic, no-frills accounts. For accounts like these, banks typically charge a monthly fee of about $3 and let you write eight to ten checks free of charge. The cost per check after that will be from 10 to 25 cents.

2. NOW and Super NOW. These are interest-bearing accounts. Regular NOW (Negotiable Orders of Withdrawal) accounts pay a set interest rate. Super NOW accounts pay a variable rate tied to prevailing market rates. Both typically carry monthly fees and per-check fees. Unfortunately, the interest rates paid are often less than 1.5 percent, and you're required to keep anywhere from $500 to $1,000 (or even $2,000 in some cases) in the account at all times. If you don't, you'll be charged a penalty fee.

"Advanced" Checking:
Money Market and Asset Management Accounts

In addition to conventional kinds of checking accounts, you may want to look at money market deposit accounts, money market mutual funds, and asset management accounts. Here are the main points to consider:

• **Money market deposit accounts.** Essentially interest-bearing checking accounts. The rate of interest changes with market conditions but is usually considerably below the actual rate paid on money market investments. Watch out for high initial "come-on" rates, large minimum-balance requirements, and limitations on the number of checks you can write each month.

• **Money market mutual funds.** About half the money market funds sold by mutual fund companies offer checking. Such accounts pay close to the actual market interest rate, and there is typically no minimum-balance requirement, no charge for checks, and no limit on the number of checks you may write. However, the smallest check you can write is usually for $100 or more, and you may not have access to your money via an ATM. Also, unless you have established a line of credit, you won't be able to draw on deposited funds until about fifteen days after a deposit has been received by the fund.

• **Asset management accounts.** Designed for active investors, these accounts usually combine a brokerage account with a money market account (which serves as an interest-bearing checking account) and a credit or debit card. The idea is to give you easy access to your money while making sure that it continues to earn a high rate of interest when you don't need it. For example, you can have your account regularly "swept" for interest and dividends, which are then collected and automatically re-invested. And you may be able to get a credit card that automatically triggers a low-interest loan against your stocks when you use it. There is also the convenience of having all of your banking and investment activities appear on a single monthly statement.

However, the smallest check you can write may be for $250 or more, and the minimum deposit amount can range from a low of $1,000 to a high of $25,000 or more. There may or may not be an annual fee of $125 or more, and unless your asset management account is offered by your bank, you will probably have to wait fifteen days before you can draw on your deposits.

F.Y.I.

One of the best ways to increase your clout with a bank is to offer to consolidate all your accounts (checking, savings, IRA, and so forth) from other institutions. Just remember that FDIC and FSLIC insurance covers a maximum of $100,000 in losses per institution in most cases.

3. Regular Checking. This is by far the most popular type of checking account. You'll pay a monthly fee and per-check charges. But, depending on the bank, there are ways to eliminate or reduce those costs. And that's where things get complicated.

Getting the Best Deal on Checking

Focus first on the monthly fee. Make sure you're aware of all the options each bank offers. Then consider playing them off against one another. Never forget that banking is a business. Everything is negotiable. So don't be afraid to ask the branch manager what he or she would be willing to do to get your business, starting with waiving the monthly regular checking fee.

Everything depends on the particular bank, but many banks will waive the fee if you arrange to have your employer directly deposit your paycheck into the account. (The same may be true if you do this with your Social Security or pension payments.) Banks may also waive the fee or offer a discount if you're a senior citizen, which many define as anyone who's at least fifty.

With some banks, you'll get a break if you agree to do without having your canceled checks returned each month, or to accept reduced-size photocopies of your checks. Other banks make it a policy not to return checks, but offer you that option for an additional fee of about $2 a month.

Just about all banks also offer some kind of minimum-monthly-balance plan as well. Generally three approaches are used:

How Do Banks Calculate Your Minimum Monthly Balance?

Leaving $100 to $500 in a non-interest-paying checking account does cost you something, of course. It costs whatever you could have earned on the money, less the tax you would have paid on those earnings. If you can earn 10 percent on $500, and you pay 28 percent federal tax on those earnings, your opportunity cost is $36 ($3 a month). On the one hand, it may or may not be worth the hassle of constantly monitoring your account. But on the other hand, such plans do insure that you will almost always have $500 or more in ready cash.

If you opt for such a plan, be sure to ask how your minimum balance will be calculated. Most people assume that the bank will add up the balance in your account at the end of each day and divide by the number of days in the month (the *average daily balance* method). But some banks use the *minimum daily balance* method, under which your account must contain the stated minimum each day of the month. Drop below the amount for even a single day and you'll be charged a fee or a penalty, or lose all interest earned (if applicable), or both.

Basically, whether the bank charges you a fee directly or earns interest on your minimum balance, one way or another it is going to get its money for providing you with checking account services.

1. Maintain a monthly checking account balance of, say, $500, and the fee will be waived for that month. Fall below it, and you pay the regular rate.

2. Keep the *combined* balance of your checking and your savings accounts at a certain minimum to avoid the monthly fee.

3. Pay different fees depending on the minimum balance you maintain. This tiered-pricing approach means that if you keep, say, $200 to $300 in the account, your fee might be $1. Keep $100 to $200, and the fee might be $2, while a balance of $0 to

$100 might be $3. Just remember that, depending on where you live, the tiered fees can be considerably higher.

Cutting Per-Check Charges

Next, turn your attention to eliminating or reducing any per-check charges. There are banks that charge $1 a month and 20 cents for each check you write. With other banks, if you keep $100 in your checking account, there will be no monthly fee and no charge for writing your first twenty-five checks. After that, each check will cost you 12 cents. But if you keep $300 in your account, you can write as many checks as you want free of charge. Per-check fees, in other words, are all over the lot.

Fortunately, there are things you can do to reduce the number and cost of the paper checks you issue:

• Arrange for your bank to automatically pay your utility bills each month (gas, water, heating oil, electricity, etc.).

• Have the bank make automatic payments on any outstanding mortgages or loans. (Agreeing to this when you negotiate the loan may reduce the interest rate as well.)

• Pay bills yourself electronically using the bank's online banking services, an increasingly popular option.

ATM Usage Fees

The location of your bank's ATMs is the next consideration. Is there a bank-owned ATM near where you work or live? If not, and if you regularly use ATMs, you may want to consider whatever bank owns the ATMs most convenient to you.

Ironically, ATMs were introduced by banks and S&Ls as a cost-saving measure. Unlike human tellers, ATMs don't earn salaries, benefits, and pensions, and they never call in sick. Customers didn't take to them at first, so massive ad campaigns were mounted by the banking industry. Once ATMs became popular, however, banks began charging for the use of their money-saving technology, and in so doing, they have been at least as creative in setting fees as they have with checking accounts.

It is thus entirely possible that the bank offering the best deal on checking in your area may be offering the worst deal on ATM transactions. The key is to make sure that you know about all the charges that may be involved.

For example, an ATM transaction may be defined as a deposit, a withdrawal, a funds transfer, a review of your current balance, a printout of the results of that review, or anything else the ATM can do. You may be allowed a certain number of free transactions per month. After that, there may be a fee for each transaction. And that's just when using an ATM owned by your bank. If the machine is owned by another institution or a nonbank third party, you will pay even more.

SMART SOURCES

Buying checks directly from your bank can be convenient, but it can also be costly. You may be able to get comparable-quality checks for half the price if you have them printed on your own. (The same is true for any printed check options offered by personal-finance programs like Quicken or Microsoft Money.) Contact these companies for price quotes:

American Check Printers
800-262-4325
www.amcheck.com

Best Checks
800-521-9619
www.bestchecks.com

Checks in the Mail
800-733-4443
www.checksinthemail.com

Current Checks
800-533-3973
www.currentinc.com

Liberty Check Printers
800-597-2435
www.libertycheck.com

Overdraft or Check-Bouncing Protection

Many banks offer a service called *overdraft* or *check-bouncing protection* for free or for a small annual fee ($25 or so). It's actually a high-interest (19 percent or more) line of credit that's activated by an overdraft on your checking account. But if you pay it off quickly, it can be cheaper than paying the bank's bounced-check charges, which are often $20 or more per check.

Minimizing ATM Fees

That's why, whenever you approach an ATM, the most important question to ask is "Who owns this machine?" If the ATM is not owned by your bank (as is usually the case with any you find in convenience stores, the mall, and other nonbank locations), you will definitely be charged a fee of some sort. The fee may be $1.50 per transaction, but in some locations it may be as high as $3 or $4 per transaction. (No wonder placing "cash-vending" machines like ATMs has become a very big, very profitable third-party business!)

There is federal legislation pending that would require financial institutions to program their ATM machines to provide you with details of any applicable ATM fees. In the meantime, if you are a frequent ATM user, make sure you are fully aware of *all* of the fees your bank charges for ATM transactions and adjust your usage accordingly.

Credit Unions, the Low-Cost Alternative

There are technical differences between banks and S&Ls, but they rarely matter to most consumers. The differences between these institutions and credit unions, however, matter very much indeed. Credit unions were established by the Federal Credit Union Act of 1934 during the

Great Depression to provide loans and banking services to people shut out by ailing banks.

The law said that credit unions could be formed by "groups having a common bond of occupation or association." And such groups were granted nonprofit, tax-exempt status, which enabled them to charge lower fees. For example, according to the *Wall Street Journal,* banks typically pay 1.5 percent on interest-bearing checking accounts, while credit unions pay an average of 2.08 percent. And most credit unions offer members free checking with no minimum balance.

Credit unions also typically charge lower interest rates than banks on most kinds of loans. Ditto for credit-card rates. Some credit unions offer cards with a 10 percent annual percentage rate (APR) and no annual fee.

For many people, doing their banking at a credit union may be the best deal going, but the usual caveats and questions apply. Thoroughly investigate the costs associated with checking. Make sure you understand the credit union's account-reporting and canceled-check procedures. Some credit unions send out quarterly (rather than monthly) account statements, and many provide just a listing of checks that have been cleared against your account (not the checks themselves).

Make sure you completely understand how the credit union deals with ATM transactions and their costs. Most credit unions do not "own" ATM machines, for example, so when you use an ATM with your credit union card, it will probably be one belonging to another institution, and there will undoubtedly be an extra fee.

Shopping for Banks: Let Your Computer Do the Walking

To find out what services your bank (or prospective bank) offers, visit MyBank on the Web (www.mybank.com). Click on a state abbreviation and then on the target bank name. That will take you to the bank's web site, where you'll find detailed information about its programs, offerings, and fees. It's a lot easier (and more informative) than picking up the phone and working your way through the bank's maze of voice-message-system menus.

Credit Unions and the Supreme Court

Finally, you should know that a change in the interpretation of the credit union law in 1982 vastly expanded the definition of who could belong to a particular credit union. Some cynics said that "if you have a pulse, you have a common bond with everyone else and therefore qualify for membership in a given credit union."

In 1998, in a suit brought by the banking industry, the Supreme Court struck down this expanded definition. (Banks pay taxes, credit unions don't, after all.) This has left the status of many credit union members in doubt and in play.

Regardless of the outcome, rest assured that no one will lose a penny. Your credit union savings are safe. And legislation has been introduced in Congress to change the law to accommodate the expanded definition of who qualifies to join a credit union.

Online Banking Options

For most people, convenience and costs associated with checking and ATM offerings are still the most important factors in selecting a bank. But a bank's online offerings are rapidly growing in importance among customers, particularly among seniors, many of whom have wholeheartedly embraced personal computers.

Lots of approaches have been tried over the past twenty years, but the model that has emerged today is for a bank to make online options available to users of the two leading personal-finance programs, Quicken and Microsoft Money. America Online's BankNow is supported by some banks as well, and others offer their own proprietary software. But most of the action centers around Quicken and Money.

Once you're set up with your chosen bank and software, you can get information on your accounts, transfer money among your accounts, pay bills without writing checks, schedule future payments, set up automatic payments, and possibly get an idea of the current value of your stock portfolio. About the only thing you can't do with online banking is withdraw cash. Unless, as a *PC Magazine* writer once quipped, "you have an exceedingly fine color-graphics printer."

Should You Bank Online?

Online banking and bill-paying are cool. No need to write out paper checks, no envelopes, no postage, no hassle. And if your bill-paying is integrated with a personal-finance program, no need to worry about record-keeping. The software will take care of that automatically.

Is it a good deal? That depends. In the future, all businesses, large or small, will be set up to accept paperless, computerized electronic funds transfers (EFTs). Today, however, even if you use EFT for many of your transactions, you still have to write paper checks to your newspaper carrier, local hardware store, and other small-business creditors. So the key question regarding online bill-paying companies is "Can you cut and mail a paper check to any of my creditors, and if so, what will it cost me?"

Some banks charge $5 to $6.50 per month to handle your electronic bill payments, while others offer the service for free. Printing and mailing paper checks may incur an additional charge. Online bill-paying is a rapidly evolving field, so you must press for the latest offerings and details.

If your bank isn't "wired," you can still pay your bills electronically by signing up with a service like CheckFree. The cost is about $10 a month, and CheckFree is supported by the leading personal-finance programs. For more information, call 800-297-3180 or visit the CheckFree web site (www.checkfree.com).

THE BOTTOM LINE

Shop for a bank just as you would any other product or service. Banks are not public utilities, after all. They're aggressive and highly competitive businesses. And, as you've discovered in this chapter, services and fees for checking accounts, ATMs, online banking, and other offerings do vary from one bank to the next.

Find a bank with ATM locations convenient to your home and office, since you'll probably be handling most of your transactions that way. If you qualify to join a credit union, by all means do so. They typically offer the lowest rates on checking accounts, loans, and other banking services.

Credit Cards and Credit Reports

THE KEYS

• Job One: Establish a credit history by borrowing money and paying it back on time.

• Use your legal right to obtain a copy of your credit report and review it for errors.

• Follow credit-reporting-bureau instructions for correcting errors in your report and take action to do so.

• Consider using credit bureaus to remove your name from junk mail and phone solicitation lists.

• Do not automatically accept any credit-card offer that comes along—shop, and shop hard, for the best deal.

Money may make the world go 'round, but credit greases the axle. People borrow money to accomplish things they never could if they had to rely on their savings. Other people lend money because they can make their money grow by "renting it out" for interest. Credit is really as essential as money, and both undoubtedly came into being at the same time.

Using Credit Wisely

Borrowing money and paying interest is an excellent idea if the money will be spent on something that will appreciate, grow, or enable you to increase your net worth. Good examples include borrowing for a home or major home improvement, your children's college education, computers and other equipment for your business, or the training you need to get a better-paying job.

But using credit to buy items or experiences—like a meal at an expensive restaurant, a vacation, or a big-screen TV—that will not help you add to your net worth is not a good idea, unless you have the money and the discipline to pay the credit-card bill in full when it arrives.

End of lecture. We covered spending and saving and the importance of eliminating (or at least controlling) credit-card debt in chapter 1. In this chapter we'll concentrate on what might be called the credit industry—how it works and how to use it to your advantage.

Establishing Credit: The Starting Point

When life was simpler, local merchants would extend credit because they knew you and your family personally. But while there are still small stores today in which you can pick up an item and say, "Put it on my account, John," as you walk out the door, try that in most places and you'll be arrested for shoplifting.

The way credit is established today is by building a history of borrowing and timely debt repayment. That's why, if you are just starting life as an adult, the best thing you can do is to borrow some money and pay it back on time. That will give you a credit record, and a favorable one at that. You can be the richest person on earth, but if you don't have a credit record of some sort, you probably will be turned down for a loan. That's simply the way the system works.

Credit-Reporting Companies

The key elements of the system are the three leading credit bureaus—Equifax, Experian (formerly TRW), and Trans Union. These companies create and maintain files on the credit histories of more than 190 million people in the United States who have a department store charge account, car loan, student loan, home mortgage, or Visa, Master-Card, or other credit cards. They also incorporate information drawn from public records, such as bankruptcies, foreclosures, tax liens, and court judgments.

What's in Your Credit Report?

Most of the information in your consumer credit report comes directly from the companies you do business with, but some information comes from public records. The typical consumer credit report includes four types of information:

• Identifying information: your name, nicknames, current and previous addresses, Social Security number, year of birth, and current and previous employers.

• Credit information: specific information about each account, including the date opened, credit limit or loan amount, balance, monthly payment and payment pattern during the past several years, and information on whether anyone else is responsible for paying the account.

• Public records information: federal district bankruptcy records, state and county court records, tax liens and monetary judgments, and, in some states, overdue child support.

• The names of those who obtained a copy of your credit report for any reason.

Some credit-reporting companies also include insurance and medical information in the reports they issue.

And they include a constant stream of current information supplied by retailers, credit-card companies, and others regarding your payment history. If you are a week late paying your mortgage in January due to holiday bills, that fact will be reported and recorded. It will become part of your credit report.

This may sound creepy. What you buy and how you choose to pay your bills is *your* business, after all! Except that it's not. Credit is a privilege, not an entitlement. No one likes the idea of having every detail of his or her financial life recorded and reported, but that's the price we all pay for the convenience of credit. And most sensible people agree that it's perfectly reasonable for a prospective lender to want to know something about you before loaning you money.

Your Most Crucial Document?

Companies that extend credit aren't the only ones that use credit reports. At some companies, it's standard operating procedure to ask for your permission to pull your credit report when you apply for a job. Landlords, insurance companies, and banks where you want to open an account may also check your credit report. All of which makes that report an incredibly important document in your life.

But what if it contains errors?

According to a 1997 *Money* magazine survey, "Of the 53 percent of Americans who have obtained their credit report, half (26.5 percent) found that it contained mistakes." Similar surveys over the years have reported similar results, although many of the errors were typographical, not factual.

With over 190 *million* people to track, credit bureaus are bound to make mistakes. Lenders know that. They know the system is imperfect. What they are mainly interested in is the overall trend. Unless a huge amount of money is involved, a blip here and there is not significant. People are interested in your overall, long-term borrowing and repayment *patterns*.

SMART SOURCES

Experian, Equifax, and Trans Union usually charge $8 for a credit report. By law, residents of Colorado, Georgia, Maryland, Massachusetts, New Jersey, and Vermont may request one free copy each year.

You can obtain a free credit report if you've been denied credit, insurance, or employment based on your credit history within the previous sixty days. If you have reason to believe that your credit report contains inaccurate information, you may also be able to request a free copy. For more information, contact the credit bureaus:

Equifax
800-997-2493
www.equifax.com

Experian
888-397-3742
www.experian.com

Trans Union
800-888-4213
www.tuc.com

Correcting Credit Report Errors

Still, the message is clear: Check your credit report before applying for a major loan to make sure that it is completely accurate. And it's not a bad idea to request a report from each of the three major credit bureaus once a year.

If you find inaccuracies, the law now requires that they be corrected within thirty days after you notify the credit bureau of the mistakes. And, once notified of an error, the bank or other business that supplied the incorrect information is required to correct its records so that the same error does not keep appearing on your credit report.

You also by law are allowed to provide credit bureaus with a one-hundred-word statement explaining the circumstances related to specific information in your report. Examples might include late payments due to an illness, a divorce-related problem, or a dispute with a manufacturer. Credit-reporting companies are required to include such statements in your credit report.

What Matters Most?

One of the most important elements in determining your creditworthiness is your track record in borrowing money and paying it back on time. But, of course, there is also the matter of how much you currently owe compared to how much you currently earn. And something you may not have thought of: your current borrowing *potential*. You might have five Visa or MasterCards with absolutely nothing on them, but if they each offer credit lines of $5,000, the credit bureaus will see that as $25,000 of potential debt and lower your score as a result.

Your score? That's right. With so many millions of people to track, credit-reporting companies have developed numerous credit scoring systems designed to neatly summarize your creditworthiness. Your income and current indebtedness are considered. But so, too, are factors like these:

• How long you've held your current job. The longer, the less likelihood that you will be fired.

• Whether you own your home and are thus less likely to skip town than a renter.

• If you rent, the length of time you've lived at the same address. This indicates stability and the ability to handle the rental payments.

• Whether you've recently applied for credit from someone else or suddenly maxed out your credit cards.

• Whether you carry balances or pay everything off each month. Lenders tend to prefer people who carry a balance since they make more money on interest payments.

• The "steadiness" of your occupation. Teachers score higher than farm workers, for example, since farm work can be seasonal. Shop owners and proprietors do not score very well because they can go bankrupt.

Not that you'll be denied credit if you have a less-than-perfect score. There is no perfect score.

SMART SOURCES

Contact these organizations for information on the best credit card deals available.

Bankcard Holders of America
524 Branch Drive
Salem, VA 24153
703-389-5445

RAM Research
P.O. Box 1700
Frederick, MD 21702
800-344-7714
www.ramresearch.com

As you may have gleaned from TV ads, nearly anyone can qualify for some kind of credit. But those with the best scores get the best interest rates, mainly because they represent the lowest risk.

Everything You Need to Know about Credit Cards (Almost)

Your credit report is relevant any time you want to borrow money, whether for a home, a car, a business, a home-improvement project, or something else. But the kind of credit most people use most often is the credit card. Some 144 million Americans have a Visa card, 93 million a MasterCard, and 41 million a Discover card. But most have little or no idea how credit cards actually work or how much money they could save if they only paid attention.

Credit-card companies make money by charging customers annual fees and monthly interest. But they also make money by charging merchants who accept the card some percentage (typically 2 to 5 percent) of the purchase. The exact percentage depends on the merchant's volume of credit-card business and average transaction size, but just about every merchant who accepts credit cards builds this cost into the store's prices. So if you pay cash, you're paying for a convenience you are not getting.

Therefore, if you can manage it, your best option is to keep your money earning interest as long as you can, use your credit card for everything, and pay all credit-card bills in full the moment they land in your mailbox.

Getting Smart about Your Credit Cards

You know the drill about using credit cards wisely. What you may not know is how important it is to actively *shop* for the best credit-card deal. Don't automatically respond to the flattering "You're preapproved . . ." direct-mail credit-card solicitations you're sure to get. In fact you should literally shred such solicitations to prevent anyone else from applying in your name (which has indeed happened). Then take an active role in shopping for a credit card the same way you'd shop for anything else.

Remember, having a lot of *potential credit* available in the form of multiple unused cards is likely to lower your score at most credit-reporting companies. So forget about going for the preapproved gold card offers you get in the mail and go for the best deal instead. And, as you'll see in a moment, it is important to keep going for the best deal since most cards today offer introductory "teaser" rates to get you to sign up and then raise you to the "real" rate after about six months.

The two leading sources of information about how credit cards compare are RAM Research Group and Bankcard Holders of America. For a fee of $4 to $5, you can get a regularly updated list of low-rate and no-fee credit-card issuers. Or you can visit the RAM Research web site, where the information is available for free.

If you go to the RAM Research site, click on "CardTrak" and then "Card Surveys." You'll be able to select among lists of cards offering low rates, no fees, and other options. In many cases, you can even apply for a card online. A recent check of Card-

SMART SOURCES

To cut down on junk mail and phone calls, send "opt-out" requests to the following credit bureaus and DMA Opt-Out Programs:

Equifax Options
P.O. Box 740123
Atlanta, GA 30374
800-556-4711

Experian Consumer Opt Out
701 Experian Parkway
Allen, TX 75013
800-353-0809

Trans Union Corporation
Name Removal Option
P.O. Box 97328
Jackson, MS 39288

Direct Marketing Association
Mail PreferenceService
P.O. Box 9008
Farmingdale, NY 11735

Direct Marketing Association
Telephone Preference Service
P.O. Box 9014
Farmingdale, NY 11735

Trak's Low-Rate Survey turned up a no-annual-fee card with an introductory rate of 2.9 percent. There were also listings for cards with rates of 6.9 to 11.4 percent and higher, with and without annual fees.

When it comes to credit cards, don't take what you're given or what you're offered. Go out and actively *shop* for the best deal. And *keep* shopping as deals and rates change.

Want a Lower Rate? Call Customer Service!

Everything about credit cards is negotiable. The industry is that competitive. For example, many banks offer introductory rates of 5.9 percent or lower for the first six months, but after that they begin charging you 18 percent or more. They may also offer you the first year with no annual fee and then begin charging you after the twelve months are up.

When either of these things happens, call customer service and explain that unless they give you a lower rate (or extend the no-fee arrangement), you'll cancel the card and go elsewhere. To bolster your argument, check RAM Research or Bankcard Holders of America beforehand for the names of banks offering cards with lower rates, and mention those names in your conversation. This will show that you're not bluffing.

It may not work every time, but if you've been a good customer and the bank has a better rate available, chances are the customer service representative will offer it to you on the spot in order to keep your business.

What's the Best Card for You?

The most important question to ask when considering the credit card deal that is best for you is whether you expect to carry a monthly balance or, like about one third of Americans, you expect to pay each credit card bill in full when it arrives.

If you promptly pay off your balance, the card's annual percentage rate (APR) of interest is irrelevant. So look for a card with no annual fee (or a very low one, like $10) and a "grace period" of twenty-five days, if possible. (You'll learn more about grace periods in a moment.)

On the other hand, if you usually run a balance, go for the card with the lowest available interest rate. And, should competing cards offer the same low rate, go with the one charging the lowest annual fee.

Remember that the real cost of a credit card comprises any fee plus the annual percentage interest rate on your unpaid balance (and the way it is calculated). Additional considerations include fees charged for cash advances and late payments.

None of this stops credit-card issuers from clouding the issue with perks and special deals. Remember, their goal is to get us into the tent because they know that most of us will never leave.

Perks: Worthwhile? Or Worthless?

The January 1996 issue of *Consumer Reports* provided a list of "worthwhile and worthless" credit card perks. It noted that some perks can be pretty expensive, since cardholders often pay for them

F.Y.I.

Paying off and cutting up a credit card you no longer use isn't enough to get it off your credit report. Unless you officially notify the card company in writing that you want the account closed, it will still appear as potential borrowing power on your credit report. A couple of months after canceling the card, check your credit report to make sure that it has indeed been removed.

Credit Repairers Beware

The Federal Trade Commission (FTC) reported in a March 1998 press release that fraudulent credit-repair firms bilk consumers out of millions of dollars each year. Typically, these firms claim that they can restore someone's creditworthiness for a fee of about $1,000 by removing negative information from a credit report. But no one can do this if the negative information is accurate and timely. In some cases, such companies advise consumers to use false Social Security numbers to establish new credit identities while failing to mention that doing so is a federal crime.

This fraud is particularly appalling because it preys on consumers who already find themselves in financial difficulty as a result of layoffs, divorce, or heavy medical expenses," says Jodie Bernstein, director of the FTC's Bureau of Consumer Protection. "Although there are legitimate, not-for-profit credit *counseling* services, the FTC has never seen a legitimate credit-repair company."

For the name of a nonprofit credit counseling service in your area, contact the Consumer Credit Counseling Service at 800-388-2227. Do *not* deal with an attorney or firm that promises to consolidate your debts in return for a percentage of what you owe. Such companies typically list themselves under "Credit and Debt Counseling Services" in the yellow pages. Stay away from them.

through higher annual fees or by having to maintain monthly balances to qualify.

Here is a rundown of the perks and extras to look for and to look out for:

• **Rental-car collision damage insurance.** Rent a car with a card offering this perk, and you can save $8 to $12 a day. If the car is damaged or stolen, this insurance will pay the difference between the total repair or replacement cost and the figure your own insurance company will come up with.

• **Airline frequent-flier miles.** Generally a good deal, but watch out for the annual fees such cards charge. By the time you have earned enough miles for a free flight, you may have paid the cost of the ticket in your annual fees. There may also be tight restrictions on when and how you can use such "free" tickets.

• **Travel accident insurance.** Buy your airline ticket with the card and get $300,000 of this kind of insurance. No problem. Flying is still the safest way to travel, so the credit card company is giving you the sleeves out of its vest.

• **Buyer protections and extended warranties.** A good idea, but mind the registration requirements. If your purchase isn't officially registered with the card issuer, you may be out of luck when you try to collect.

• **Rebates.** The Discover card is the leader here. But everything is tiered. There is no annual fee, but to get the best rate of interest—currently 17.4 percent—you must charge $1,000 a year on the card. Otherwise your interest rate will be 19.8 percent. And, to earn the full 1 percent rebate, you must charge $3,000 or more each year. Oil companies, car manufacturers, and many other firms offer rebate deals, too.

The Fine Print: How Is Your Balance Calculated?

RAM Research and Bankcard Holders of America make it exceptionally easy to identify cards with

F.Y.I.

Ever wonder about the meaning of all those numbers on your credit card? The first six digits identify the company that issued the card. (Numbers beginning with 34 or 37 are American Express, 300–305 are Diners Club, 4 are Visa, 51–55 are MasterCard, etc.) The next four numbers correspond to the geographical region and branch office. The next five are your account number. And the last one is a "check digit" included for extra security.

Building and maintaining a good credit history is more important today than ever before. Companies use that information to make decisions about everything from loaning you money, to insuring your life and property, to offering you a job. So it just makes good sense to understand what's in your credit report, and to make a point of checking it regularly for errors and omissions that might impact your creditworthiness.

With a strong credit rating, you'll be in a good position to demand (and get) the lowest rates and fees offered by credit-card companies. Use RAM Research or Bankcard Holders of America to identify the best ones, but make sure you understand all the card's terms and conditions—including how your balance will be calculated—before you sign up.

no-fee/low-fee and low-interest-rate offerings. And the credit limit of any given card will be determined when you apply (based on your application and credit report).

But what about the way interest charges are calculated? Credit-card issuers must disclose this on the back of your billing statement, but most people don't pay attention. And that can be a costly mistake.

Most banks use the *average daily balance* (including new purchases) method of calculating your interest charges. They average each day's debt and charge you interest on that amount. However, instead of counting your purchase from the day it is posted to your account, some banks start the interest clock from the day you made the purchase.

In addition, if you carried an *average daily balance* of $1,000 on your card in March and paid all but $1 of it, you'd get an unpleasant surprise in your April bill. Because you did not pay the March bill in full, the bank will charge you interest on your average daily balance for that month. That average balance, of course, will be close to $1,000.

On the positive side, some banks still give you a *grace period* for new purchases. That means that if you pay your new balance in full by the due date, they will not charge you interest on any of the new purchases you made during the month.

Finally, you will probably want to avoid any card that uses the *two-cycle average daily balance* method for calculating your interest. Under this method, if you pay in full one month and carry a balance the next, you'll be charged as if you had carried that balance for both months.

CHAPTER 4

....

Buying or Leasing a Car

THE KEYS

• Buy a car with your head, not with your heart.

• Do your homework on the dealer's cost before going in to buy.

• Bargain from the dealer's actual cost up, not from the sticker price down.

• Insist on treating your trade-in as a completely separate transaction.

• Leasing may be the low-cost way to get behind the wheel, but not to stay there.

• Shop around for auto insurance, and make sure you buy enough liability coverage.

Buying a car may be second only to having a child when it comes to cutting a hole in your pocket. Just think of the expenses: gasoline, oil, tires, state safety inspections, insurance, maintenance and repairs, interest on your auto loan or lease. And then there's depreciation. Want to see $4,000 disappear in an instant? Just buy a $20,000 car and drive it off the dealer's lot. The typical new car loses between 20 and 35 percent of its value during the first year you own it.

Still, cars and kids are not something most of us would want to do without. So, with due acknowledgment of the costs of car ownership, the question becomes how do you find the car that's right for you, and then get the best deal when you're ready to buy?

Finding the Right Car

The best advice in looking for a car (or a van, minivan, pickup, sport utility vehicle, etc.) is to shop with your head, not with your heart. Automobile companies have spent billions to convince you that "you are what you drive." Well, you aren't, of course. But it's still difficult to counteract the emotional appeal. There you are, a fighter pilot flying down the freeway in your hot new sports car, checking your sleek instrument panel and maybe even using a cellular phone headset to communicate with your base. "I'll take it!" you say. "Just tell me my monthly payment."

It's quite human to be emotional about your car. So don't sweat it. But do admit it. That way you'll be ahead of the game. Car salespeople are very good at detecting such vulnerabilities and not at all above using them against you. As long as you're aware of what's going on, your brain can intervene and prevent you from making a costly, impulsive decision.

Using *Consumer Reports*

As for identifying models of interest, you can't do better than *Consumer Reports.* Each April, this magazine publishes an issue devoted to automobile ratings and profiles, crash-test results, reliability studies, and reports on the best and worst used cars. Much of the same information is included in *Consumer Reports Buying Guide,* a book that's issued each year. Unlike many other sources of car reviews, *Consumer Reports* does not accept advertising.

You can find these publications at your local library. Or you can go to the magazine's web site (www.consumerreports.org) and get what you need there. The cost is $2.95 a month or $24 a year ($19 if you subscribe to the magazine). The site is searchable, so if you want to look at reviews and repair records of the Ford Taurus Wagon and the Subaru Legacy Wagon, for example, you can call up just those two reviews and print them out.

Arming for Battle

Most people say they hate negotiating for a car, which is why GM's Saturn unit has led the way in offering new cars at a fixed price, and why Circuit City's CarMax unit has tried the same approach with used cars. However, at this writing, studies

SMART SOURCES

Most people think of the American Automobile Association (AAA) as a source of travel information and road service and repair. But many local and regional "Triple A" organizations also offer members a complete car-buying service, including dealer cost information on new cars, reports on what your old car is worth on the current market, and lists of places you can take a used car to have it gone over by a mechanic. In some cases, your Triple A will have negotiated with local car dealers to get them to offer members their best prices.

"Let me tell you something," says Jerry, the manager of a GM dealership. "If selling cars were so profitable, you'd see a lot more big national companies getting into it.

"You've got all the taxes and expenses of any other retail store. And it can cost you $200 or more a month in interest just to keep a vehicle on the lot.

"And you should see what *customers* try to pull. Just the other day a woman traded a car she said had only 19,000 miles on it. Then we learned that the actual mileage was 119,000 miles. We asked her for $1,500 to compensate. So she hired a lawyer.

"Our industry is far from perfect. But it isn't all one-sided. There are far more dishonest consumers than there are dishonest dealers. At least, that's my perspective."

indicate that the jury is still out on the success of the fixed-price, no-negotiation approach, either for the industry or for the consumer.

More than likely, if you want the best price on a new or used car, you're going to have to negotiate. That means being forced into a game you have no idea how to play, let alone how to win, against a professional who plays it every day. This is what people hate. Most Americans are not at all shy about insisting on the best quality at the best price when dealing with products and services they understand. But most of us don't understand the car business.

First, no dealer is going to voluntarily reveal what's known in the industry as the *dead cost* of a car—the actual dollar cost to the dealer for the make, model, and features you want to buy. Why? Because for every smart person who knows enough to start with the dead cost and bargain up, there are probably nineteen others who will start with the sticker price and try to bargain down. The dealer may realize a profit of only $300 to $500 on a deal with a knowledgeable buyer, but make $1,200 or more on the nineteen others who don't know any better. Why give that up?

Invoice, Holdbacks, Backend Money, and Incentives

Car dealers are certainly entitled to a fair profit. However, it's not your job to determine what's fair and what isn't. Your job is to come as close as you can to estimating the dead cost of a car and seeing how little above that the dealer will accept.

Dealers have all kinds of reasons for wanting

to make a sale. There are regional contests (with prizes). There are numerical quotas entitling them to better prices from the factory. And there is the interest on the money the dealer has tied up in each car. If money is tight, a dealer might be willing to sell you a car for what hc's got invested in it, just to free up the cash. But obviously no one can afford to do that on a regular basis.

One way to find out what the dealer paid for a car is to use the *Consumer Reports* New Car Price Service. For $12, you can get a report that includes the invoice price (what the dealer was billed) and the sticker price (what they'll try to make you pay) for a given car and all available options and special packages, plus current consumer rebates, factory-to-dealer incentives, and holdbacks.

For $10 more you can get a verbal quote, updated daily, on the trade-in value of the car you're currently driving. Call *Consumer Reports* at 800-933-5555 for more details. (Unfortunately, there's no service in Canada.)

If you have access to the Internet, however, there are even easier ways to get the information you need free of charge. Each of the following sites offers dealer cost, incentive, holdback, and pricing information:

• Edmund's Automobile Buyer's Guides (www.edmunds.com)

• Kelley Blue Book (www.kbb.com)

• AutoSite (www.autosite.com)

• Microsoft's CarPoint (www.carpoint.msn.com)

SMART DEFINITIONS

Backend
The less obvious area of dealer profit, including financing, insurance, extended warranties, and other add-ons.

Holdback
A markup of 2 to 3 percent added by the factory and included in the invoice price of a vehicle. The dealer does indeed pay the invoice price, but as cars are sold, the factory rebates the holdback amount, usually quarterly. Holdbacks provide a built-in profit for the dealership, which can advertise a car at "$1 over invoice price" and still make several hundred dollars on the sale.

SMART DEFINITIONS

MSRP
Manufacturer's suggested retail price (the "sticker price").

ACV
Actual cash value, or wholesale value, of the car you're trading in.

How to Calculate Dead Cost

To calculate your starting point, take the invoice price and subtract the holdback, the backend money, and the customer cash/rebate. The result should be close to the dead cost of the vehicle. This is where you begin. If you're buying a new car, don't allow the salesperson to draw you into a discussion about trading in your old car or how you'll be paying. Keep the focus on the price at which the dealership will sell you the car you want. Tell the salesperson that you can't possibly discuss anything else until the two of you get that nailed down.

Begin by making it clear in writing what car you want and exactly how you want it to be equipped. You can even fax your specifications to most dealerships instead of bringing them in in person. Offer $300 over what you've calculated to be the dead cost of that car and see what the dealer says.

If you can get the car for between 2 and 5 percent above the actual cost to the dealer, you will have done well. Be prepared to go up to $500 over on most domestic cars in good supply, and $800 to $1,000 over for imports and some domestics with a strong current demand. For hard-to-find or specialty cars, you may have to pay $1,500 or more over the dealer's actual cost. Once again, you're starting from the dead cost, not the car's invoice here. And, most importantly, you know the game.

What about charges for destination fees, advertising or sales promotion, and dealer prep?

Destination charges are usually not marked up and count toward the dealer's cost. Advertising and promotion charges, often from $200 to $400 per car, should be negotiable. After all, if the car has just arrived on the lot and no ads have been run, no money has been spent advertising that particular car. In any case, ask to see documentation before agreeing to pay this charge. As for dealer prep, the factory is already paying the dealer to ready the car for sale, so it's pure dealer profit. Refuse to pay it.

Finally, don't be impressed if the salesperson offers to sweeten the deal by "throwing in" a $300 rust-proofing package, paint sealant, fabric protection, extended-service contract, or alarm system. You should refuse to even consider such add-ons since they are invariably grossly overpriced. Rust-proofing, for example, actually costs the dealer about $30. A full-featured alarm system that the dealer prices at $600 actually costs closer to $200. And a couple of cans of Scotchgard will let you apply your own fabric protection.

How to Bargain

Once you've decided on the make and model you want, the question becomes one of which dealer can get you the car in the color you want with the equipment you want at the best price. If the car you want isn't in your local dealer's showroom, the chances are he can get it from another dealer, even if that dealer is located hundreds of miles away. Car dealers swap cars with one another all the time. Having a dealer order precisely the car you want from the factory is another possibility.

The moment of truth arrives when you are ready to make a deal and schedule an appointment with your sales representative. At this point, the salesperson will figure that the battle is just about won. If you're interested enough to begin

SMART SOURCES

See car expert Jeff Ostroff's chatty, irreverent online book, *How to Buy a New Car* (zim.com/ejo/gm.htm), and check these web sites:

Fighting Chance
www.fightingchance.com Tracks changes in the prices of car options. The package is $25 for the first model and $8 for each additional model, and includes the current number of days' supply in inventory, the number of units dealers are currently selling per month, and other valuable information.

CarInfo.com
www.carinfo.com Created by Mark Eskeldson, author of *What Car Dealers Don't Want You to Know* and other books, this site is particularly strong on revealing the latest scams having to do with buying, leasing, and repairing cars.

SMART DEFINITIONS

F&I Department

The car dealership's finance and insurance department. Here the salesperson is called the "business manager." He or she may try to sell you all kinds of expensive but often worthless add-ons. Resist!

Upside down

Owing more on the car you want to trade in than what it's worth.

Factory-to-dealer incentives

Often called "backend money." They are not publicized and can range from several hundred to several thousand dollars. So, even if you pay "$150 over factory invoice," the dealer is probably making a lot more than that on your deal.

talking, you obviously want to make a deal. All that remains is to work out the details.

That's where your research comes in. Car salespeople are not accustomed to encountering well-informed consumers. That's why it is a good idea to begin the discussion by taking control. Start by presenting your offer in a very businesslike way. Give the salesperson a copy of your research and a copy of any spreadsheets you may have created to evaluate the purchase.

Say, "By my estimate, this is the dead cost of that car. If you'll sell me the car for $X over that cost, I'll sign the papers now." Start with a value of X equal to 2 percent of the dead cost and see what the salesperson says. If the salesperson refuses, respond with "Well, how much above this figure did you have in mind?" Once the salesperson names a figure, you have your bargaining range.

Be prepared to come up, but make the salesperson work for it. As in, "Well, I could come up another $200 if you'd be willing to throw in the rust-proofing package." You know that the package is worth only about $30, but the salesperson doesn't know that you know. Nor does the salesperson know that you realize the dealership has got to make a profit and probably will never sell the car for 2 percent above cost. Suggesting a quid pro quo like this gives the dealership the profit it needs but gets you a free rust-proofing package into the bargain.

Buying a Car Online

According to J. D. Power & Associates, 16 percent of new-car buyers used the Web for shopping in 1997, up from 10 percent the year before, And according to a J. D. Power director, by the year 2000, "half of all new-car buyers will use the Internet in the shopping process."

Or, as Richard W. Everett, director of strategic technologies for Chrysler's sales and marketing operations, told the *Wall Street Journal* in late 1997, "In a very short period of time, the last stupid customer is going to walk through our dealership doors."

So what about online car-buying services? Each has its own approach and its own user interface, but the overall goals are the same. The idea is to smooth and facilitate the nuts-and-bolts interaction between you and a car dealer. Typically, you'll be asked to enter your zip code first. Then you will have the opportunity to select the make, model, features, and equipment you want. (You may be asked about your trade-in, but, as explained elsewhere, you should treat this as a separate transaction. So don't mention it on your electronic form.) Your specifications and contact information are then sent to a dealer in your area, which will contact you with the firm's sales offer within forty-eight hours.

In theory, the dealer's offer will be his or her best price. After all, conventional advertising costs can run from $300 to $450 per vehicle, while the dealer's payment to an online buying service may work out to as little as $70 per car. And there are no sales commissions to pay. So a dealer *should* be able to offer you a car for less when you buy online. (The most successful dealers establish separate online departments staffed with employees who are paid a salary instead of a commission.)

On the other hand, none of the Internet-based car-buying services offers any kind of guarantee that the prices quoted by their member dealers are the lowest you can find. Member dealers do not have to sign a contract swearing to offer the absolute lowest price. All they have to do is pay the $500 to $2,500 a month each of the online shopping services charges to get referrals.

To their credit, many online car-buying web sites offer free resources for calculating dealer cost, and most encourage you to take advantage of them. But in the end, these are just souped-up referral services.

Not that there is anything wrong with that. But consider the big picture. In the best of all possible worlds, you would buy your Toyota from the dealership nearest you at the best possible price and take it there for all service and maintenance. You would thus have a relationship with one of the merchants in your area, and, assuming it is a good relationship, that merchant would "take care of you." He or she would go the extra mile, free of charge. Pleased with the service you received, you would recommend the merchant to friends and relatives. That merchant wants to keep you happy because he or she wants you to buy your next car from the store.

This really is how good car dealers think. Haggling with a salesperson makes you queasy? Okay. Take full advantage of the Internet-based car-buying services listed here to get "best-price" offers from dealers in your general area (fifty miles or less). There is no cost or obligation. Then take the offers to your nearby dealer and ask if he or she can do any better.

No need to bring out the dealer-cost reports. No need to negotiate. "Here is what these guys will charge me for this car with this equipment. But I'd really like to buy from you, my neighborhood dealer. Naturally, I plan to have the car serviced here. So, can you give me a better deal?"

Clean and simple. No pressure. In almost every case, your local guy will find a way to beat the proffered deals by a hundred bucks or so.

Ultimately, there are many ways to play the car-buying game, and the Internet has added many more. The key thing to remember is that nothing is carved in stone and that if you actively engage in the process, you will not only save money, you will probably have a lot of fun. Assemble all the information you can, but don't be a nasty tightwad. You have to let people make a living.

Taking the long view, it might well be worth it to you to pay $200 more to get your car from a local dealer with whom you want to establish a relationship than to save two hundred bucks by driving one hundred miles to pick up a car from a dealer you will never see again.

Trade-Ins and Financing

The best way to buy a car is to negotiate your deal and get it laid out in writing. Then, and only then, indicate that you will be paying cash for the car. Slap a FOR SALE sign on your present car, park it at the end of your driveway, and get a loan for your new car from your local bank or credit union. In this way you will get the best deal on your new

Car-Selling Web Sites

Auto-By-Tel
www.autobytel.com
Started: 1995
Dealers: 2,700
Offers new and used cars through dealers who pay up to $2,500 a month for *exclusive* referrals. Financing, leasing, and insurance products are available. Accepts no advertising.

AutoWeb
www.autoweb.com
Started: 1995
Dealers: 2,100
Channels referrals to *multiple* dealers, each of whom pays $25 per referral. Financing, leasing, and insurance products are available. You can list your used car for $19.95 per month.

Microsoft CarPoint
www.carpoint.msn.com
Started: 1997
Dealers: 1,095
Refers buyers to multiple dealers, each of whom pays up to $1,600 a month. No financing or insurance products are offered at this time. The used-car database is supplied by Reynolds & Reynolds.

SMART MONEY

According to Andrew Brosnan, a former car dealership manager, "Dealers write numbers they don't want you to know, like the profit on the deal or the value of your trade-in, in a simple code. They use the first nine letters of the alphabet to represent the numbers 1 through 0. A equals 1, B equals 2, and so on. So if you see 'CJJJ' written on a trade-in appraisal sheet, you'll know that, regardless of what the dealer may say, you're actually getting $3,000 for your trade-in.

"This is one area where dealers will really underestimate you. They'll use these codes in plain sight on the paperwork, even on the documents they hand you to review."

For more insights and tips, visit Mr. Brosnan's web site: www.autoadvice.com.

car, the best price for your old car, and the best interest rate on your car loan.

Unfortunately, most people don't have this kind of flexibility. And selling a used car yourself is a hassle—placing ads; appointments made, canceled, and missed; waiting for a prospective buyer to sell his or her current car; and on and on. For most people, it's much more convenient to sell the car they're currently driving to a dealer.

Take Your Used Car Out of the Equation

Just be aware that regardless of how they structure things, dealers will never actually pay you more than the current wholesale value of your car. If you sell it yourself, on the other hand, you will get closer to its retail value. The current wholesale/retail values of automobiles can be found in *Edmund's Used Cars* (www.edmunds.com) and the *Kelley Blue Book* (www.kbb.com), available at your local library and newsstand, as well as on the Web. You might also check the National Automobile Dealers Association (NADA) guides for your region. Your banker or credit union loan officer probably has a copy.

One of the worst things you can do is to agree to make your trade-in part of your car-purchase deal. Car salespeople will try to get you to do this because it gives them another tool to use to confuse you. But stop and think: Why should selling your old car have anything to do with buying your new car?

If you want to get the most for your current car, do your research, and drive around to the dealers in your area asking each what they would be willing to pay you for the car. Sell it to the highest bidder, clean and simple. You'll get the wholesale price, but you won't have the hassle of selling it yourself.

Dealer Financing?

Many times, most of the profit a dealer makes on a car deal comes from selling the financing. Here's how it works. When you agree to dealer financing, the dealership will send your credit information to the various banks and lenders it does business with. Along with an approval, these institutions will respond with the dealer's *buy rate* for your loan. The buy rate is the lowest interest rate the bank will offer the dealer for your financing. But the car dealer can mark this up significantly.

Let's say you need to finance $20,000 for five years and the buy rate for your loan is 8 percent. The dealer can mark that up to 10 percent and keep the additional money. The extra 2 percent adds about $20 to your monthly payment and ends up costing you $1,200 *extra* over the course of the loan, all of it pure profit for the dealer.

To put it another way, suppose someone said, "I will pay you $1,200 to spend the time to fill out a loan application at your local bank and to tolerate a few delays as you buy your new car." Doing the paperwork and making the effort can save you big bucks in the end.

On the other hand, there is no law requiring

Auto Loans at a Glance

• Auto loans are similar to personal loans, but with a lower interest rate because the car serves as collateral.

• Terms runs from three to five years for new cars, less for used ones.

• Rates can vary by 1.5 percent or more within the same town, so it pays to shop around.

• Processing (or document) fees can run from $20 to $200 if the fee is based on the loan amount.

• If you are required to insure the car for theft and fire, shop for the insurance before simply buying it from the bank.

• Ask if the interest rate will be lower if you agree to have the bank automatically deduct your monthly payment from your account.

you to accept the first interest rate the dealer offers. Because car dealers do so much business with lenders, they get buy rates that are lower than just about any rate you could get yourself. And they deal with lenders who appreciate the importance of speed in getting a deal done, something your local bank may not be concerned with.

So here's a tip: Shop for an auto loan first to find the best rate you can get as a private individual. Then, when the subject of dealer financing comes up as you complete the deal, ask for that rate. At the very least, the dealer will profit from the difference between the buy rate and the rate you could get on your own. And the dealer will be inclined to accept your offer in order to maintain control of the deal. No need to wait for you to go shopping for a loan from some third party.

Ideally, you will get the same loan at the same rate you would have gotten from a lender, but by going through a dealer, you will get it much faster and with a lot less hassle.

Leasing Basics

Leasing a car is often the cheapest way to put yourself behind the wheel of a new (or even used) car. But it is rarely the least expensive way to stay there. Lease payments are lower than car loan payments because you're paying for the car's depreciation during the term of the lease, not for the car itself.

Most consumer car leases are "closed-end" leases, meaning that at the end of the lease, you can buy the car for the residual or "guaranteed" value. If your car turns out to be worth more than

Leasing Tricks and Traps

A car salesperson's job is to get as much money out of you as possible, and every new element you add to a deal offers yet another opportunity to do so. Let's say you decide that leasing is for you and sit down to do the paperwork. All of a sudden you're facing additional charges for "conveyance," "disposition," "acquisition," "preparation," and the like. Say what? "Oh, don't worry," you're told, "we'll just roll them into the lease."

Like fun you will! Charges like these are pure dealer profit, and they are completely negotiable. To give yourself the leverage you need, bargain with two dealers at once and play them off against each other.

Second, watch the "capitalized cost" listed in the lease agreement. Some dealers are not above letting you negotiate the price down all you want and then filling in the car's sticker price in the lease contract. The capitalized cost of the vehicle should be the price you negotiated based on dead cost and dealer profit, plus taxes and incidental fees like maintenance agreements. If that amount is not filled in on the lease agreement, the dealer is trying to pull the wool over your eyes.

Third, it happens all too often: Consumers think they're signing a purchase contract, but, because the salesperson has artfully positioned his or her hand over the document title, the consumer ends up signing a lease agreement instead! You can avoid this by insisting on holding the documents in your hand and reading them before signing.

this figure, you might want to buy it from the company, sell it yourself, and pocket the difference. Otherwise, you can simply walk away.

Lease or Buy?

From a purely financial standpoint, you should buy the best car you can afford, maintain it, and drive it for seven to ten years or more. After all, once your loan is paid off, use of the car itself is "free" since

Being Smart about Leasing

Generally, you'll owe 8 to 15 cents for every mile you drive over 12,000 to 15,000 miles a year. If you typically drive more miles per year than specified in the lease, buying that "excess" mileage in advance as part of the lease will be cheaper than paying for it when you turn in the car.

Don't sign a lease for a longer term than you expect to drive the car. If you sign a five-year lease and want to get out of it after three years, you may face a hefty "early termination deficiency" charge. So that everything is clear, ask the dealer how much you will owe at the end of each year if you decide to end the lease.

Be sure to get *gap insurance*. You are responsible for your own car insurance, but if the car is wrecked or stolen, your insurance company will pay you only the current depreciated value of the car, a sum that will probably be lower than what you owe on your lease. Without gap insurance, you'll be responsible for that difference.

you now own it. If you're in the market for a truck for your business, or you're in sales and feel you need to drive an expensive car to impress clients, a lease is worth considering because it may allow you to deduct a greater portion of the vehicle's cost from your taxes. Otherwise, leasing is rarely cheaper than buying and is usually more expensive than financing.

Aside from the business angle, leasing may make sense for your particular situation. Here are some examples:

• You have no car to trade and not enough money to make a down payment on a new or used car.

• You have the down payment but can earn more than 10 percent a year by investing it elsewhere.

• You need lower monthly payments.

• Your current car is worth less than you owe on it, giving you "negative equity." By including your current car in the deal, your negative equity can be made part of the lease amount. When you pay off the lease, you can walk away owing nothing on your current car.

• You're well off, want to drive a new car, and view the never-ending monthly payments as part of your cost of living. For an extra fee of $25 a month or more, the dealer/lessor will do all the maintenance and give you a loaner when the car is in the shop.

You *Must* Have Car Insurance

Regardless of how you buy your car, regardless of whether it is new or used, you must have car insurance. You'll need to shop around for the best rates, of course. Premiums for the same insurance can vary by thousands of dollars from one company to the next, and your challenge is to find the company that offers the best deal for your particular situation.

You can begin with over-the-phone quotes from GEICO (800-841-3000) and Amica (800-992-6422). Both firms get consistently high ratings from A. M. Best, the well-known insurance industry analysts. By selling directly to consumers, they're able to offer exceptionally good service and coverage at very competitive rates.

SMART DEFINITIONS

Capitalized cost
The price you have negotiated for the car, not the invoice price, the sticker price, or anything else.

Money factor
The interest rate.

Residual value
The leasing company's best guess at what the car will be worth at the end of the lease.

For a small fee, you can use the *Consumer Reports* Auto Insurance Price Service (800-224-9495) to do the legwork for you. Tell them the makes and models of your cars, answer a few questions (drivers in your household, driving records, annual mileage, how much coverage you want), and they'll produce a report listing up to twenty-five of the lowest-cost policies available for your household. The report costs $12 for one car and $8 for each additional vehicle that you ask about in the same call. It's currently available in eleven states: California, Colorado, Florida, Georgia, Illinois, New Jersey, New York, Ohio, Pennsylvania, Texas, and Washington.

What You're Buying

Car insurance policies consist of three components: collision/comprehensive, medical payments, and liability. Here's a brief explanation of each one:

• **Collision/comprehensive.** This is the simplest since it essentially pays for any physical damage done to your car as a result of fire, flood, theft, and accidents. Once you've paid off your car loan or bought out your lease, it's often best to drop this coverage or to increase your deductible.

• **Medical payments.** This coverage takes care of your doctor and hospital bills and those of any of your passengers injured in an accident, up to a specified dollar amount. You may also hear it referred to as personal injury insurance or no-fault insurance.

• **Liability.** Also known as bodily injury liability and property damage liability, this is the biggie, often accounting for more than half of your car insurance premium. In forty-two states and Washington, D.C., drivers are required to maintain a certain level of liability insurance. In other states, you're required to post a bond if you are involved in an accident.

Liability insurance covers you and your family and other drivers who are using your car with your permission. If your savings are nil and you do not own a home, get coverage of at least $100,000 per person, $300,000 per accident, and $100,000 for property damage. If you own a home and other major assets the injured parties can go after, you will probably be better off buying an "umbrella liability policy," offering coverage beyond any auto or homeowner's liability insurance you may have. Umbrella liability policies often provide more coverage for less money than separate home and auto liability policies.

F.Y.I.

According to *Consumer Reports,* if you're a typical driver, you'll pay $5,800 or more for car insurance during the time you own your car.

Saving Money on Insurance

In addition to shopping around for the company that's right for you, here are several other ways to save money on your car insurance premiums:

1. Increase your deductible. You can probably save 15 to 25 percent a year by raising the collision and comprehensive deductible from $250 to $500.

2. Insure your cars and your home with the same company. Many insurance companies offer multi-vehicle discounts (cars, boats, recreational vehicles), so be sure to ask. And you can almost always get a better deal if you give your car and homeowner's insurance business to the same company.

THE BOTTOM LINE

When you're dealing in thousands (and even tens of thousands) of dollars—as is the case with a new car— there's lots of room for negotiation. In fact, buying a car may be among the most nego- tiable purchases you'll make. The truly smart car dealers will give you a fair deal with no tricks because they realize that by doing so they earn your loyalty for your next car purchase, and because they know you will tell your friends of your good experience.

Just be smart. Do the research on the dealer's actual cost— and don't forget insurance premiums when figuring what you can afford.

3. Buy a conservative car with all the latest safety equipment. Allstate and State Farm publish annual lists of the cars for which they charge extra because of unusually high insurance claims. And they each publish another list of cars that get a price break. Find out what category a car is in before you buy it.

4. Maintain a good driving and claims record. If you've been accident- and/or claim-free with your current company for several years (typically three), you may qualify for a preferred rate of as much as 20 percent off what you're now paying.

5. Reduce your annual mileage. If your annual mileage goes down dramatically because of, say, a move or job change, check with your insurance company to see if you qualify for a lower rate.

6. Park in a garage. You may be able to save as much as 20 percent on your premiums if you reg- ularly park your car in a garage.

7. Stop smoking. Insurers in some states offer nonsmoker discounts.

8. Take advantage of "young retiree" discounts. Some companies offer a 10 percent discount to peo- ple who take early retirement. That's because they've found that, as a group, early retirees spend less time on the road, pay their premiums promptly, and generate very few claims.

CHAPTER 5

Putting a Roof over Your Head

THE KEYS

• The bank or other lender will determine how much house you can afford, so pay attention to their formulas and rules.

• Surprise: Your real-estate agent works for the seller, not for you!

• If you have a good credit history, it pays to really shop for your mortgage.

• Pay attention to mortgage types and terms. They do make a difference.

Housing is among the biggest expenses in the budgets of Americans. And, of course, the expense depends on the type, quality, and location of the place you choose to call home.

Home Ownership and the American Dream

"This is my land. This is my house. And, within certain broad community restrictions, I can do whatever the heck I want to do with it." Others have phrased it more felicitously, but at bottom, that is the essential sentiment in the land of the free and the home of the homeowner. Owner-ship—at least individual ownership—was never a part of the ethos of the Native American, but the promise of land for the common man was the engine that built the United States. That's why, to this day, owning a home is such a deeply embed-ded part of the American dream.

It's also the reason why buying a home usually makes good financial sense for most of us. First, the federal government has long encouraged home ownership through provisions in the tax code. The interest you pay on your home mort-gage loan each month is tax-deductible. The rent you pay to your landlord is not.

The Costs of Ownership

On the other hand, owning your own home is rarely inexpensive, something prospective first-time buyers need to consider. When you're ready to settle down, get married, start a family, or otherwise decide that you'll be staying put for the next five years or so, it probably makes good sense to buy rather than rent. But, leaving aside expenses like closing costs for now, consider these costs of owning a home:

• Real-estate taxes. Typically paid to the city, town, county, and township for services and to support the local school system. Usually several thousand dollars a year.

• Homeowner's insurance. (See chapter 6 for details on figuring what you need and what it will cost.)

• Heat, water, electric, and sewer fees.

• Trash disposal.

• Lawn care, snow removal, and other seasonal maintenance.

• House painting every five to ten years.

• Security system fees and mandatory fees paid to any local homeowners' associations.

Whatever you've calculated as the cost of living in a given house, the actual figure will be higher. Water pipes develop pinhole leaks, air conditioners die, the furnace won't light, the driveway needs to be resurfaced, the roof leaks. . . . To paraphrase Francis Bacon, "He that owneth his own home hath given a hostage to Fortune." One way to avoid, or at least minimize, major surprises is to hire a licensed building inspector to examine the property before you buy it. Nevertheless, you can be certain that owning your own home will always cost more than you think.

How Much House Can You Afford?

The first step in the house-hunting process is to figure out what the bank or other mortgage lender will decide you can afford. You may be willing to live on peanut-butter sandwiches and ice water to make the monthly payments on your dream home, but the bank won't see it that way.

Nearly every aspect of the home-mortgage market today is the result of the fact that most lenders package their mortgages into bundles and sell them on the secondary market. Since the biggest buyer in this market is Fannie Mae, its requirements have become the de facto standard.

The Mortgage Lenders' Formulas

Following Fannie Mae guidelines, lenders typically apply two tests when determining how much you can borrow on a house:

1. If you make a 10 percent down payment, your fixed housing costs—principal, interest, taxes, and insurance (also known as PITI)—should not exceed 28 percent of your total gross (before taxes)

monthly income. If you make a 20 percent down payment, the total can be as large as 32 percent.

2. Assuming you plan to make a 10 percent down payment on the house, your credit card, car loan, student loan, and other monthly debt payments *plus* PITI should not total more than 36 percent of your gross monthly income. If you can put 20 percent or more down, banks will adjust this debt-to-income ratio upward.

If your down payment is less than 20 percent, not only will the 28/36 percent tests apply, you will probably also have to buy private mortgage insurance (PMI). This can add a quarter to a third of a percent a year to your loan. Fortunately, many lenders will let you drop your PMI once your down payment and principal payments bring your equity to 20 percent. But be sure to ask. Many lenders "forget" to remove this charge when you get to 20 percent equity, although legislation has recently been introduced in Congress to make it mandatory that they do so.

Finding an Agent

Once you've gotten a sense of your price range, it's time to go look at some houses. Don't do so with the thought of buying at this point. Just try to get an idea of the kinds of properties in your area that fall into your price range. There are a number of ways to locate properties that are for sale:

• **Advertisements.** Classified ads in newspaper, Yellow Pages listings, and free real-estate publications

SMART SOURCES

When choosing a home inspector, insist on one who is a member—not just someone who "follows the standards"—of the American Society of Home Inspectors (ASHI). For a list of members in your area, call ASHI at 800-743-2744.

available in racks at your local supermarket or convenience store are easy places for a good start.

• **Real-estate company web sites.** On some top-notch sites, you can search by price range, location, and special features. And when you find a property of interest, you can often view several color photos, detailed specifications, and even a floor plan. To get the address of a local agency's web page, check their ads in the real-estate section of the newspaper or simply call them on the phone.

• **MLS books.** Most real-estate agencies are members of an organization called the Multiple Listing Service (MLS). Each month, this organization publishes a large book containing the photos and specifications of houses listed by member agencies in the area. You can visit any MLS-member real-estate office and page through the latest edition. If the office you visit won't let you look at the book until you have an agent, tell them you can easily go to another MLS-member agency that doesn't impose that requirement.

Three Ways to Look at Houses

One painless way to look at properties is to watch for open houses. Typically held on the weekend, open houses give you a chance to walk through a property pretty much on your own. A sales agent will be in attendance, of course, and you'll be asked to sign the guest book. But you are not required to do so.

At the other end of the spectrum is the "For Sale by Owner" property. To look at one of these houses, you'll have to make an appointment and tolerate the slight discomfort of the owners presence as you traipse through the house. More than they'd like to admit, real-estate agents owe their existence to the awkwardness of this situation. The agent insulates you so completely that you probably will never see the owner unless you do decide to buy the house and end up meeting across a table to sign the final papers.

The third option is to hook up with a real-estate agent or salesperson. Real-estate agents work for brokers, who own and run the office. Both are licensed by the state. Those who use the designation *Realtor* on their business cards are also members of the National Association of Realtors, a trade association that promotes high ethical and professional standards (www.realtor.com).

What to Know about Real-Estate Agents

It may come as a wake-up call to many home buyers, but real-estate agents don't work for you. They work for the seller. Indeed, surveys by the Federal Trade Commission and others have shown that between 70 and 74 percent of home buyers are confused about just whom their real-estate agent represents. This is no accident. A seasoned agent may act as if he or she works for you. An agent may, for example, encourage you to reveal the highest price you're willing to pay and the size of the down payment you plan to make. What most people don't know is that the agent is obligated to pass along that information to the seller. So don't reveal it!

STREET SMARTS

Sandra, a single mother of two, says, "Have the house professionally inspected before you sign anything or put down a deposit.

"I found my guy in the yellow pages under 'Home Inspection,' and he charged $250. One of the first things he did was turn on the central air-conditioning unit—in winter. It didn't work.

"He said a new air conditioner would cost about $1,500. I figured the sellers would be willing to replace the unit or reduce their price by that amount. They weren't. I was so upset that I told my agent that I didn't think I wanted the house after all.

"As it turned out, the air conditioner was replaced. Only later did I learn that my agent had given up part of her commission to make the deal go through! Apparently this kind of thing happens all the time."

Many agents also promote the notion with sellers that whatever commission they quote (typically 5 to 8 percent of the sale price) is standard and nonnegotiable, and they get the seller to sign a contract to that effect. In reality, the fee is quite negotiable. They may also encourage the sellers to price their home at a level that will insure a fast sale, when that may not be the sellers' top priority.

How Agents Are Paid

Real-estate agents make the most money on a sale if they serve as both the listing and the selling agent—they enter into a contract with the sellers to sell the property and they personally find a buyer. In such cases, the agent typically splits the percentage with the broker. So on the sale of a $250,000 home with an agreed-upon commission of 6 percent ($15,000), the agent and the broker will each make $7,500.

Things get more complicated when a property is listed by an agent at one real-estate agency and sold by an agent at another. Usually, the two companies split the fee and divide up their portions internally. The key point is that it is in the agent's best interest to try to sell his or her *own* listings first, and those listings may or may not be ideal for you and your family. Regardless of who listed a house, it is always in the agent's best interest to get you to pay the highest possible price.

That's why you should be cautious when the agent tries to control your opening bid. "They're asking $300,000, but I think they'll take $280,000. Would you like to make an offer?" In the absence of this kind of "guidance," you might have suggested an opening offer of $265,000 or $270,000.

How to Figure Your Mortgage Payment

There are several quick and easy ways to get a handle on monthly mortgage payments. You can use personal-finance software packages like Quicken, Microsoft Money, or Managing Your Money, all of which include "mortgage calculator" features. (See chapter 1 for contact information.) If you don't have a computer, you can buy (or borrow from the library) a book of amortization tables. Or you can use the table shown here, which offers a brief subset of what you'd find in one of these books for a fixed-rate, thirty-year loan at interest rates ranging from 6 to 10 percent.

Mortgage Payment Table

Monthly principal and interest for a fixed-rate thirty-year loan.

Loan Amount	6.0%	6.5%	7.0%	7.5%	8.0%	8.5%	9.0%	9.5%	10.0%
$ 10,000	$ 60	$ 63	$ 67	$ 70	$ 73	$ 77	$ 80	$ 84	$ 88
20,000	120	126	133	140	147	154	161	168	176
30,000	180	190	200	210	220	231	241	252	263
40,000	240	253	266	280	294	308	322	336	351
50,000	300	316	333	350	367	384	403	420	439
60,000	360	379	399	420	440	461	483	505	527
70,000	420	442	466	489	514	538	564	589	615
80,000	480	506	532	559	587	615	644	673	702
90,000	560	569	599	626	660	692	725	757	790
100,000	600	632	665	699	734	769	805	841	878
110,000	660	695	732	769	807	846	885	925	966
120,000	720	758	798	839	881	923	966	1,009	1,054
130,000	780	822	865	909	954	1,000	1,047	1,093	1,141
140,000	840	885	931	979	1,027	1,076	1,127	1,177	1,229
150,000	900	948	998	1,049	1,101	1,153	1,208	1,262	1,317

Note: For mortgages over $150,000, just add the appropriate figures. For example, to find the monthly mortgage payment for a $200,000 mortgage at 7.5%, add the amounts shown for $150,000 at 7.5% ($1,049) and $50,000 at 7.5% ($350) to get $1,399.

Should you say as much to your agent, you might receive a weak smile and hear, "Well, if that's what you really want to do." Real-estate agents are obligated to take any offer you make to the seller. But there is nothing to prevent them from suggesting that your offer is ridiculously low. Don't let this tactic rattle you. If the sellers reject the offer, you can always go higher. Who cares what they think? After all, the sellers probably don't know any more about the market than you do, and they may be very eager to consider any offer at all.

Since you don't buy a house every day, you are naturally at a disadvantage. So you must rely on your real-estate agent in most cases. Just remember that "your" agent really works for the seller, and that everything is negotiable.

Mortgage Shopping

As soon as you begin to think seriously about buying a house, you should get copies of your credit report. (See chapter 3 for details on credit reports and how to contact the three major credit bureaus for yours.) Review the reports carefully for errors. Do they show that you still have accounts that you know you have closed? Do they show any late payments that you can prove you made on time?

Next, look for a lender. Possibilities include:

• Commercial banks

• Credit unions

• Savings banks and savings and loan associations

• Mortgage companies and mortgage brokers

• Home builders and developers

• Federal and state housing agencies (Fannie Mae, Freddie Mac, and others described in this chapter)

Using a Mortgage Broker

One increasingly popular option is to work with a *mortgage broker.* In years past, mortgage brokers were used primarily by people who had such bad credit histories that they couldn't get financing any other way. No more. Today, mortgage brokers have become professional mortgage shoppers and facilitators. And more and more people are using them, both for obtaining a first mortgage and for refinancing.

Banks and other lenders give mortgage brokers special rates because they, in effect, serve as sales representatives. They also handle all the paperwork. You will want to check rates in your area, but in general, it should not cost you any more to go with a mortgage broker than to look for a loan on your own. Mortgage brokers are paid by the lender, so you should be suspicious of anyone who tries to charge you any special fees for his or her services.

For additional information, call the National Association of Mortgage Brokers in McLean, Virginia (703-610-9009), or visit their web site at www.namb.org.

Nothing Is Impossible!

"The mortgage market today offers consumers an incredible array of choices," says Barry Zigas, a senior vice president of Fannie Mae. "And no one considering purchasing a home should make any assumptions about what isn't possible." For example, in some counties, if your household income does not exceed $66,500, you can make a down payment of just 3 percent and borrow up to $227,150, thanks to a Fannie Mae program. The Federal Home Loan Mortgage Corporation (Freddie Mac) has similar programs.

The Federal Housing Administration (FHA) insures loans of up to $170,362 on single-family homes with no income limitations and as little as 3 percent down. Similar programs for qualified veterans are offered by the Department of Veterans Affairs (also called the Veterans Administration or VA). And your state probably has a housing agency offering low-interest mortgages with minimal (or even no) down payment requirements.

Adjustable Rate or Fixed?

If you have a sterling credit record and a stable employment history, you can usually pick and choose among various mortgage products. There are two main questions you'll have to ask yourself: Should you go with a fixed or adjustable rate? Should you pay the loan back over a term of fifteen or thirty years?

Fixed-rate, thirty-year mortgages are the most common. The money is paid back over the term of the loan, and the interest rate and monthly payments never vary. With an adjustable-rate mortgage (ARM), in contrast, the interest rate and monthly payment amount can vary within certain defined limits. Here are the key concepts you need to know about ARMs:

• **Rates.** An ARM's interest rate is pegged to a certain rate—called a *benchmark*—like the One-Year Treasury Constant Maturity rate or the Cost of Funds rate of the Federal Home Loan Bank board's 11th District (California, Arizona, and Nevada). Or something else. Lenders will charge a certain number of percentage points—usually about three—above these benchmarks.

• **Teasers.** Artificially low *teaser rates* are often used to attract borrowers. The teaser rate may actually be lower than the current benchmark, and it is often two to three points lower than the rate on a fixed-rate loan. But teaser rates last for only a limited period of time, usually one to three years.

• **Periodic adjustments.** Lenders typically adjust the rate once a year, but most ARM agreements stipulate an annual cap limiting the number of percentage points by which the rate can be increased in any given year. Thus, if the cap is two points and the benchmark rate to which the loan is pegged rises three points, the lender can increase your rate by only two points. In the following year, however, the lender can increase your rate another two points if the benchmark rate remains high.

• **Overall cap.** Be sure your ARM includes a cap limiting the percentage points your rate can be increased for the life of the loan. At this writing, an overall cap of six points is common.

SMART MONEY

You may have the option of hiring a *buyer's broker* (or *buyer's agent*). Unlike the traditional real-estate agent, a buyer's broker represents you in the purchase of a house. They do everything a traditional agent does, but they are motivated to look out for *your* best interests, not the seller's.

A buyer's broker may be paid a percentage of the sale price, a fixed fee, an hourly rate, or a combination of all three. According to *Money* magazine, "Buyers average a 5 percent savings when represented by a buyer's agent rather than a sales agent." The main drawback is that you will probably be required to sign an agreement requiring you to use a given buyer's broker exclusively for a set period of time.

SMART SOURCES

The Real Estate Buyer's Agent Council (REBAC) is the largest association of real-estate professionals focusing on this area. For the name of a buyer's broker in your area, call them at 800-648-6224 or visit the REBAC web site at www.rebac.net.

ARMs are usually a good idea if you need a lower monthly payment in the first few years to be able to qualify for the house you want. They are also likely to be the cheaper alternative if you plan to stay in the house for only four or five years. That's because the teaser rate may not expire until the third year.

But they are not without risk. If interest rates rise and your income doesn't, you could find yourself in a financial bind. That's why it's a good idea to ask yourself if you can afford the highest allowable rate on the ARM before choosing that option. If you can't, then you should opt for a fixed-rate mortgage instead.

Of course, nothing is forever. Some ARMs offer you the right to convert to a fixed-rate mortgage at some time in the future without paying closing costs again. But lenders may charge you an extra up-front fee or raise your interest rate by a fraction of a percent as a result. In general, you're probably better off doing without an expense like this and refinancing (replacing it with a new mortgage) down the road if rates do happen to drop.

Should You Get a Thirty-Year or Fifteen-Year Mortgage?

Paying off the mortgage and truly owning their homes is a goal for millions of people. Unfortunately, from a financial standpoint, it's not always the smartest thing to do. That's why, even if you can afford the higher monthly payments that come with a fifteen-year mortgage, you may be better off with a thirty-year term.

Start with this fact: The best investment most people can make is to put as much money as possible into a tax-deferred retirement plan, whether it's an IRA, Keogh, 401(k), or something else. These are pre-tax dollars that get invested and are allowed to grow, compounding their gains year after year tax-free. Taxes are paid only after you begin to withdraw your funds, at which time you will presumably be retired and in a lower tax bracket.

In general, most people should pay off their credit cards and car loans, put as much money as the law allows into tax-deferred investments, and only then think about paying off the mortgage at a speeded-up rate. Keep in mind that mortgage payments are made with *after-tax* dollars. So if you're in the 28 percent tax bracket, you'll have to earn $1.40 for each dollar you put toward paying down your mortgage ($1.40 less 28 percent equals $1.00).

Also, because home-mortgage interest can be deducted from your gross income when figuring your federal tax, if your mortgage rate is 8 percent, the rate you are actually paying may be closer to 5 percent (again, assuming you are in the 28 percent tax bracket). For more on taxes and tax brackets, see chapter 10.

From a financial standpoint, paying off debt is just like investing. So in this example, you are effectively "earning" 5 percent on whatever money you pay to reduce your mortgage. If you took that same amount of money and used it to pay down your credit-card debt, you would "earn" 18 percent (or whatever rate you are currently being charged by the credit-card company). If you put the money into some taxable investment, you might earn 10 to 15 percent or more.

And here's a real kicker: If you've got kids, you're sure to be concerned about paying for college. When it comes to qualifying for financial aid, your retirement savings are not counted as an asset. But at many schools, the equity you have built up in your home *is* considered an asset. So the faster you pay down your mortgage, the wealthier you appear to college financial aid officers.

A Word about Points

As a product, nothing is purer than money. A dollar is worth a dollar, regardless of when a given paper bill was printed. There is no question of model year, excess mileage, wear and tear, or what's fashionable and in demand this season. Money is *always* fashionable.

So, unlike the price of a car or a house, the price you will pay to borrow a dollar by taking out a mortgage will vary within a narrow range. And that price is usually a combination of your interest rate and *points*. A *point* is 1 percent of the amount you are borrowing. Points are paid by you as an upfront lump-sum fee when you agree to the loan.

This seems like an unnecessary complication. Think of it instead as a means of adding flexibility.

Again, money is money, so the price you yourself, with your credit history, employment record, and assets, pay to borrow a set amount to buy a given property is going to be essentially the same, regardless of the lender. It's just a question of how and when you pay that price.

For example, one mortgage lender may offer you a rate of 7.75 percent and one point, while another may offer 8 percent and no points. In the end, both loans will cost you an almost identical amount of money, but you'll be paying it in different ways.

Without doing a lot of heavy number crunching, if you have diligently shopped for a mortgage by contacting established, reputable firms and come back with several varying offers, you can assume that they are all going to be very close in terms of total cost over the term of the loan.

The main variable is you. If you plan to stay in your house for seven or more years, it may make sense to pay the points and get a lower monthly payment. If you're going to be out of there in three years, you should opt for the no-point deal at a slightly higher interest rate and higher monthly payments.

The Buying Process

As is appropriate in a book about personal finance, this chapter has zeroed in on the financial aspects of buying a home. But what about the actual process. Real-estate laws, regulations, and procedures are primarily a state matter, so the details will vary depending on where you live. But here are the main steps you will take once you've found a house you think you want to buy.

Step 1: Making an Offer

You tell your agent that you'd like to offer a certain amount of money for the house. The agent takes your offer to the seller, who either accepts or rejects it. If your offer is rejected, you can move on or sweeten your offer

If it is acceptable, you will be asked to provide a *binder* or *earnest money* to secure your offer. The typical amount is $1,000, and if the deal goes through, it counts toward the purchase price.

SMART SOURCES

Here's how to contact the various federal and state agencies mentioned:

Fannie Mae
800-832-2345
www.fanniemae.com

Freddie Mac
800-373-3343
www.freddiemac.com

Federal Housing Administration
Contact a lender or check the federal government section of the phone book for the HUD office.
www.hud.gov

Veterans Administration
800-827-1000
www.va.gov

State Housing Agencies
Check the state government section of your local phone book, or contact the National Council of State Housing Agencies (202) 624-7710
www.ncsha.org

Step 2: Inspection

The gross price establishes a starting point for negotiating the details. As the prospective buyer, your next step is to have the house gone over by a qualified building inspector. House inspectors have a totally different perspective than you do. They know what to look for, and they certainly are not in love with the property. Hire them. Listen to their advice. And make your purchase decision with open eyes.

Step 3: Negotiating

This is the tough part. For example, suppose your inspector discovers a leak in the roof. The cost of fixing that leak can easily be determined by getting two or more estimates from licensed roofing firms in the area. Should that cost be deducted from the price you are willing to pay for the house, or should the present owners have the problem fixed without reducing their price?

As the buyer, learn all you can, state all you want. Then see what the sellers say. They want to sell. You want to buy. There should be a deal in there somewhere.

Step 4: Going to Contract

That deal will eventually be codified in a *contract*. And it is here that you must be most careful. Everyone talks about the *closing* or *settlement*—the final meeting when all the papers and checks (lots of checks) are signed to complete the sale. But the underpinnings of the deal can be found in the sales contract.

The contract or *agreement of sale* is really the main event. That's why it can be very important to have an attorney review it to make sure it protects your interests before you sign.

When to Refinance?

At this writing, mortgage rates are down, and banks and other institutions have plenty of money they are eager to lend. That very well may change in the future, but regardless of what happens, if you currently have a mortgage, it is smart to keep an eye on interest rates and to periodically consider refinancing—replacing your existing mortgage with one offering a lower interest rate.

The old rule of thumb for determining whether refinancing was likely to be worthwhile was called "2-2-2." If you had been in your home two years, intended to stay at least two more years, and could get an interest rate two points below your current loan, then refinancing would probably save you more than enough money in lower monthly interest payments than you would pay in refinancing points and fees.

Today, according to Neil Bader, chief executive of the Skyscraper Mortgage Company in New York City, a drop in mortgage rates of even half a percentage point can justify refinancing if the related costs are wrapped into the loan. Such loans are sometimes called "zero cost" refinancings. They are possible because, in return for about three eighths of a point in the rate, all fees are paid by the mortgage broker or lender.

So, do not automatically assume that refinancing won't save you money, even if the new rate is only a little lower than what you're currently paying. Instead, find a mortgage broker in your area whom you trust—ask your friends for recommendations—and then simply call and ask him or her to evaluate your situation. And don't hesitate to call back the next time interest rates drop.

Step 5: The Deposit

The deposit may be as little as 5 percent or as much as 10 percent of the purchase price. That can be tens of thousands of dollars due months before you complete the actual deal, so be sure to plan for it. The money goes to an escrow agent, who will usually place it in an interest-bearing account.

Make sure that the agreement says your deposit will be returned to you in full if the sale has to be canceled because you are unable to get a mortgage.

The Final Step: The Closing

The closing or settlement finalizes the deal. Your lender and real-estate agent will alert you to the various checks (and amounts) you will have to write at settlement, but nothing can prepare you for the actual experience of doing so.

Certainly it is fair to ask you to compensate the seller for a pro-rated share of any real-estate taxes he or she may have already paid. Same with sewer, electric, water, and any other pro-rated fees. But $1,000 for title search and insurance on a home that has had only one owner? Lawyer's fees of $300 to $600 or more? And $800 to the state for "transfer tax"? (What did the state do to earn a rake-off on a home sale?)

The final total for your closing costs can be breathtaking. In fact, as a general rule of thumb, you can expect it to be between 5 and 7 percent of your mortgage. So if you're borrowing $200,000, your closing costs, including points on your loan, might be as much as $14,000. You will be alerted to this fact beforehand, but you need to be prepared. You need to decide whether it is in your best interest to pay the fees in cash or to roll them into your mortgage loan (assuming you're offered that option).

THE BOTTOM LINE

Be realistic about how much house you can afford, and then really shop for your loan. If you have a good credit rating and not too much credit-card debt, you're probably the kind of customer a lender is looking for.

Remember, the real-estate agent typically works for the seller, not for you. So be careful how much information you reveal. In some parts of the country, buyers' brokers are becoming popular alternatives to traditional real-estate agents because they represent you and your interests.

Finally, keep in mind that a home is probably the biggest single purchase you will make in your life. As difficult as it may be, don't let yourself be driven by your emotions.

CHAPTER 6

....

Home-owner's Insurance

Owning a home is the foundation of the American Dream. And certainly for most of us, our homes are the largest single asset we will ever own. That's why it's so surprising that, according to Marshall & Swift, a leading collector and publisher of building cost data, nearly two-thirds (66 percent) of American homes are *under-insured* by an average of 35 percent.

Replacement Cost

To put that into dollar terms: If the home you bought five years ago for $250,000 were to burn to the ground, the chances are that you'd have to borrow $87,500 to make up for the portion of the replacement cost your homeowner's insurance policy does *not* cover.

Actually, the shortfall could be more or it could be less. On the one hand, although it was part of the purchase price, the land your home sits on doesn't figure into its replacement cost. On the other hand, building and materials costs will certainly have increased since you bought your home. But even if the shortfall is in the neighborhood of $30,000, it will come as a very nasty surprise—a surprise that could be avoided for relatively little money.

Figuring Replacement Cost

The fundamental question is "How much will it cost to rebuild my house if it's totally destroyed?" Keep in mind that this cost has nothing to do with the price you paid for the house or what you could sell it for today. Nor is the value of the land a factor. The main considerations are local construction costs, your home's features, and the quality of materials used.

If your home was built relatively recently as part of a typical housing development, it's probably safe to rely on your insurance agent's estimate of its replacement cost. You can also verify that estimate quite easily. Simply calculate the number of square feet in your home and multiply that figure by the building cost per square foot for your type of house in your area. Real-estate agents, builders, and professional appraisers will be able to supply the dollars-per-square-foot figure you need.

If you live in an older home that was custom-built or that's been improved over the years with significant additions like a deck, a gourmet kitchen, a new master suite with walk-in closets and a Jacuzzi—if it is, in effect, unique—it may be worth spending the $200 or so that a professional appraiser will charge to visit your home and prepare a written estimate of its replacement cost. Among other things, appraisers will be aware of any major changes in community building codes that might increase the cost of rebuilding your house.

What to Look For

Once you have a handle on your home's replacement cost, it's time to consider the type and amount of insurance you can afford. If you've just bought the house, your bank or mortgage lender probably made certain that you also bought enough insurance to cover the amount of your

F.Y.I.

Homeowner's insurance is not terribly expensive. According to a survey conducted by the Alliance of American Insurers, owners of homes valued at $125,000 or more paid about $300 to $600 in 1991 for their homeowner policies. Even if you double those amounts to account for inflation and for higher-priced houses, the figures involved are quite small compared to the protection (and peace of mind) you'll get in return.

F.Y.I.

It's a good idea to notify your insurance agent—in writing—whenever you make major additions or improvements to your home, or whenever you buy or inherit expensive items like Oriental rugs, antique furniture, silverware, works of art, or valuable collections (coins, stamps, and so forth). Your agent can then review your policy and tell you whether you need to increase your coverage.

mortgage. And you may very well have increased that amount to cover your down payment as well.

But as we've said, the key issue is not what you paid for your house to begin with—whether you bought it last week or five years ago, what's important is, what would it cost to rebuild *today?*

Automatic Inflation Protection

Chances are, if you've lived in your house for more than a year, the amount of coverage you signed up for originally has been increased annually to keep pace with inflation. Most homeowner policies include an *inflation-guard clause* that automatically boosts both the amount of coverage and the annual premium to account for the current rate of inflation. That's a genuine convenience, and it's worth checking to make sure your policy includes it.

Replacement-Cost Coverage

But covering yourself against inflation might not be enough. What if construction costs in your area go up faster than the rate of inflation? What you really need is a *replacement-cost policy* that takes into consideration both inflation and the cost of rebuilding.

Replacement-cost policies go way beyond the "HO-3" coverage considered by many to be the minimum that most homeowners should buy. With a replacement-cost policy, the insurer promises to replace your home. But there's a catch. Replacement-cost policies specify a particular dollar amount or *face value,* but they also contain caps that limit your reimbursement to 20 to 50 percent over that face value. If your policy has a face value of, say, $150,000 with a 20 percent cap, and the estimate to rebuild your house is more than $180,000, you'll have to come up with the difference.

That's why an even higher level of insurance exists. It's called *guaranteed-replacement-cost* coverage. With a policy like this, the insurer promises to pay the full cost of replacing your home, no matter how much money is involved. If you can afford it, this is probably the kind of coverage you should buy.

Whether you buy replacement-cost or guaranteed-replacement-cost coverage, make sure the policy includes language specifying that damaged property will be repaired or replaced with materials of similar kind and quality. There should be no deduction for depreciation due to age or wear and tear.

And you should make a point of asking your agent what happens if future ordinances, building code changes, and other regulations boost the dollar cost of replacing your home. You may need what's called an *ordinance and law* endorsement to cover that possibility.

Additional Living Expenses

What if your house is so badly damaged by a fire or one of the other "covered perils" listed in your homeowner's policy that you have to move out while repairs are made? In all likelihood, your insurance company will help you with some of the cost of doing so under your policy's *additional living expenses* clause.

F.Y.I.

Inflation has averaged 3.1 percent a year for the past several decades. But residential construction costs in the United States increased by 5.5 percent in 1997, according to industry analysts Marshall & Swift. Indiana experienced the greatest increase, with construction costs up 7.9 percent (more than double the average rate of inflation) over the previous year.

Degrees of Coverage: HO-1 through HO-8

Homeowner's insurance is regulated by each individual state. Fortunately, all states have adopted the same set of designations for levels of coverage:

HO-1. "Basic" homeowner's. Protects against eleven named perils (fire, lightning, windstorms, theft, and so on). Considered so limited that many states are phasing it out.

HO-2. The "broad" policy. Covers seventeen named perils, including falling objects, weight of snow and ice, frozen pipes, and damage caused by faulty electrical and heating systems, among others.

HO-3. The "special" policy. Costs 10 to 15 percent more than HO-1, but protects against "all perils" except those that are specifically excluded (flood, earthquake, nuclear accident, war, and others). Most people should view H0-3-level coverage as their starting point.

HO-4. The renter's policy. Protects personal possessions against the seventeen perils named in the "broad" (HO-2) policy. Play it safe and pay any extra that may be charged for liability protection as well.

HO-6. Co-op or condominium owner's insurance. Covers personal property and liability, but not the structure. It is assumed that the building will have its own policy.

HO-8. For people unable to obtain or afford guaranteed-replacement coverage on an older home. Covers the eleven perils named in the HO-1 policy and promises to repair the damage (but not necessarily using the same quality materials), or pay you the actual cash value of your home, less depreciation.

Note the word *additional* here. What your insurance company will typically cover are reasonable and necessary *increases* in your household's normal living expenses while repairs are being made. They might cover the cost of a renting an apartment or staying at a "residence inn," for example, but you'd be expected to buy groceries and cook your own meals.

Be aware, too, that some homeowner policies set limits, often expressed as a percentage of the coverage on the house itself. The policy may specify, for example, that you'll be reimbursed for "additional living expenses up to 20 percent" of your house coverage. So if your house is insured for $150,000, you'd be reimbursed for a maximum of $30,000 of additional living expenses, which may or may not be enough to get you through the ordeal.

What about Earthquakes and Floods?

Most homeowner's insurance policies specifically exclude earthquakes and floods as covered perils. While you can usually add earthquake coverage as an endorsement to your policy, the cost may increase your premium by as much as 50 percent. Surprisingly, wood-frame houses cost less to insure than those built of brick, and much depends on the historical frequency of quakes in your area.

Flood insurance is something else altogether. You can buy it from most insurance companies, but it's subsidized by the National Flood Insurance Program (NFIP) and managed by the Federal Emergency Management Agency (FEMA). If you live in an area that has been flooded in the last one hundred years—or even the last five hundred years—your mortgage lender will almost certainly insist that you purchase flood insurance.

SMART SOURCES

If you need flood insurance, there's a good chance you can buy it through the same company that handles your homeowner's policy. Start by calling them and ask if they write flood insurance through the National Flood Insurance Program (NFIP). If not, they can probably recommend another agent in your area who does. Or you can call the NFIP toll-free response center (888-225-5356, ext. 445) and ask for assistance in locating an agent.

Beware the 80 Percent Rule

The rule of thumb used to be that you should insure your home for 80 percent of its replacement cost because houses are rarely ever totally destroyed. But graphic TV-news coverage of the devastating effects of recent disasters like Hurricane Andrew and the Oakland, California, fire of 1991 has made a lot of people question the old 80 percent rule. The fact is, if disaster strikes, you *can* lose everything.

The good news is that you'll probably find that adding, say, $20,000 to $30,000 of coverage to a $150,000 home costs only an additional $50 to $100 a year. For that amount of money, and considering the downside risk, it simply makes good sense to insure your home for the full 100 percent of its estimated replacement cost.

The average flood insurance premium is $308 a year for $85,000 worth of coverage. You should insure your home for 100 percent of its replacement cost and buy enough additional insurance to cover the contents of your home. Either that or move to higher ground.

Liability Protection

Once you've got the replacement-cost element nailed down, the next point to take up with your insurance agent is liability coverage. Fortunately, it's no longer necessary for most people to buy liability coverage separately. Most of today's homeowner's (and renter's) insurance policies include liability insurance of some sort. And it is far more important than you might imagine.

If a door-to-door salesperson, or your next-door neighbor's child out selling Girl Scout cookies, slips and falls on the morning dew while approaching your front door, you can be sued. It doesn't matter that you did not invite either one of them to come to your home. Nor does it matter that no reasonable person would expect every homeowner to mop up the dew each morning on the off chance that some unexpected visitor might approach the front door.

To put it another way: Today, anyone can sue anybody over anything. Right, wrong, common sense, and personal responsibility do not enter the legal equation. Lose the case and the plaintiff's lawyers can take everything you have ever worked for or own. Win the case and you could still be facing a mountain of legal bills.

Most policies include $100,000 to $300,000 of liability coverage, but that may not be enough, depending on your net worth. Awards of a million dollars are not uncommon, in which case you might have to come up with an additional $700,000 or more to satisfy the judgment. How? By selling your assets.

Therefore, make sure that the liability amount specified in your policy covers, at a minimum, the financial value of your assets. And better still, *double* the value of those assets. If you operate any kind of business out of your home—as a growing number of people do—be sure to discuss the liability issue with your agent from that perspective as well.

Umbrella Insurance

If your assets are substantial—you own an expensive home and cars and have accumulated a sizable investment portfolio—you may need what's called *umbrella* or *excess liability insurance* on top of

STREET SMARTS

"I was devastated when the diamond pin I inherited from my grandmother was stolen," says Angela. "But the blow was softened when I remembered that I'd had the pin appraised several years ago and included in my homeowner's insurance policy on a special rider."

Items like jewelry, watches, coin collections, and other exceptionally valuable items are typically excluded from coverage for loss or theft, *unless* you buy a rider that specifically names the item and insures it for a given amount. The cost of the rider—also known as a *personal-articles policy*—will be about $1.50 per $100 of coverage. It should itemize the insured item, including its appraised value.

the liability protection provided by your home-owner policy. Umbrella insurance is generally sold in increments of one million dollars, but don't let that number scare you. You can probably add a

How to Shop

As with any major purchase, it pays to shop around for homeowner's insur-ance. The same policy may vary in price by as much as 50 percent from one insurance company to another. There are three ways to buy homeowner's insurance:

• **Shopping by phone.** For competitive rates on homeowner's insurance, call American Express (800-535-2001), Amica (800-242-6422), or GEICO (800-841-3000). They sell directly to consumers and thus avoid the expense of agents' commissions. If you're associated with the U.S. military, try USAA (800-531-8080).

• **Working with an independent agent.** An independent agent or broker sells policies for several insurance companies and can help you find the one that's right for your situation. Another advantage to dealing with an independent agent is that he or she will typically represent you in your dealings with an insurance company. Ask friends (or your real-estate agent) for recommenda-tions, or check the yellow pages of your local phone book.

• **Buying from an exclusive agent.** State Farm, Allstate, and Farmers Insurance Group are the three largest home insurers. Their policies are sold through their own insurance agents, and you can find them in the yellow pages.

Before settling on a particular company, it's also a good idea to check up on its financial strength. Several independent organizations (A. M. Best, Standard & Poor's, Moody's, among others) rate insurance companies. You'll find the ratings in most public libraries. Or you can call the National Insurance Consumer Helpline (800-942-4242) and ask them how to contact the insur-ance department in your state to find out about a company's ratings and complaint history.

one-million-dollar umbrella policy to your existing homeowner's insurance for about $200 a year.

If you were to be hit with a major lawsuit—exceeding the $100,000 to $300,000 of liability coverage in your homeowner's policy—the umbrella policy would "open up" and provide you with an additional one million dollars of liability coverage.

Insuring Your Stuff

Personal-property insurance is another standard component of homeowner's and renter's insurance policies. As the comedian George Carlin might say, personal property is your "stuff"—your furniture, stove, microwave oven, VCR, TV, stereo, and so forth.

Generally, personal-property coverage is set at about 50 to 75 percent of the value of your house. If you're a renter, you'll have to calculate a dollar amount. In fact, whether you're a homeowner or a renter, it's a good idea to spend some time in each room of the house—including the attic and basement—and make a list of all the items of value. You may be surprised at just how much all your "stuff" is worth.

There's no need to be meticulous. You're after two things. First, a rough estimate of the replacement cost of the items in your home. Second, the identification of any special items—pieces of jewelry, artwork, collectibles, and so on—that need to be called out and specifically insured by adding a rider to your policy.

Next, consider a *replacement-cost guarantee.* Most policies reimburse you for what you could sell an item for, given its age and depreciation—not for what you'd have to pay to replace it. If the policy

SMART MONEY

Don't assume that your landlord's policy covers anything at all. And make a point of finding out what it *does* cover before you sign the lease. According to data published by the Independent Insurance Agents of America (IIAA), insuring your possessions as a renter can cost as little as $100 a year. But make certain your policy includes liability insurance. In all probability, the landlord's liability coverage will specifically exclude any accident that occurs in your apartment.

you're considering doesn't include a replacement-cost guarantee, ask about adding it as a rider.

Finally, be sure to document your belongings. Take photographs, or better still, videotape your possessions. Get a friend to run the camera and follow you around as you walk through each room, opening closets and drawers and describing important items—how you got them, what you paid for them, and so on.

Save the receipts for the big-ticket items, record their model and serial numbers, and store this information along with any appraisals and your visual documentation someplace other than in your home—like in a safe-deposit box.

There are no guarantees, but the more evidence you can produce in the event of a loss, the greater the likelihood that your insurance company will pay you an amount sufficient to cover the loss. Insurance companies are not evil. They believe in the concept of shared risk. But people do attempt to defraud them. So your goal must be to collect—and protect—all the evidence you can of your home and its contents.

Ways to Cut Costs

Insurance is a gamble. But if you take steps to increase the odds in favor of prevention or early detection of a disaster or mishap, many insurance companies will reduce the cost of your premiums. Here are some of the things you can do that may help you qualify for discounts:

1. Install double-cylinder locks on your doors, deadbolt locks on your windows, and iron bars beneath any skylights. Also install security for your attic, basement, and garage entrances.

2. Install smoke detectors and fire extinguishers. Better yet, install a centralized alarm system that automatically notifies the alarm company in the event of a fire or a break-in. Installing such a system may cost $1,500 or more, but it could cut your premium by 15 to 20 percent.

3. Boost your deductible to the max. The highest, best, and most economical use of insurance is to pay for catastrophes, not to smooth out every little bump on the road of life. The standard deductible (the amount you pay before the your coverage kicks in) is $250. But couldn't you probably afford $500, or even $1,000 or more—particularly if doing so reduces your premium by 12 to 24 percent?

4. Opt to pay your premium annually, since it may be cheaper than paying quarterly or semiannually.

5. Quit smoking. A good idea in any case, but one that can reduce your homeowner's insurance substantially. That's because 23,000 residential fires a year are caused by smoking, according to the Insurance Information Institute.

6. If you have a second home, use the same insurance company to insure both. You'll want to look into the details, but this should eliminate the need to pay for liability coverage on both properties.

7. Consult your insurance agent before you begin building a home or second home. Believe it or not, the construction methods used by your builder may have an impact on your future homeowner's insur-

SMART DEFINITION

Rider

According to *Black's Law Dictionary*, Fifth Edition, a rider is "a schedule or small piece of paper reflecting an amendment, addition, or endorsement annexed to some part of a roll, document, or record." In laymen's terms, riders, "floaters," or "endorsements" are customized additions to standard contracts. The insurance contract may say "all contents of your home," but with a rider you can specify "including my Cartier diamond brooch with its assessed value of $X." This leaves no doubt but that a specific item is covered. Not incidentally, riders make it possible to customize a document without having to completely redraft it.

ance costs. For example, your builder may be planning to staple the roof shingles because that method is cheaper than nailing them on. But if your insurance company offers a discount for homes with the shingles nailed in place, you may want to change the building plans.

8. If you are at least fifty-five and retired, you may qualify for a homeowner's insurance discount of up to 10 percent. That's because seniors tend to spend a greater part of the day in and around their homes, which serves as a deterrent to thieves. It also increases the likelihood that someone will be on hand to call in a fire alarm at the first sign of smoke.

Health, Life, and Disability Insurance

When you buy a house, you're required by the bank or mortgage lender to show that you have homeowner's insurance to cover the property against catastrophic losses. But at no time in your life is anyone likely to require you to buy health, life, or disability insurance. That may be unfortunate, since these kinds of insurance policies are as important to you and your family as property insurance is to a bank.

How to Buy/Evaluate Health Insurance

Most companies large and small provide their employees with health insurance as part of the standard benefits package. You may even have the option of choosing among different plans and providers. If you're self-employed or work for a firm that does not offer health insurance, you'll have to shop for a policy. In any event, it pays to review your options and to understand the two major types of health insurance: traditional indemnity (or fee-for-service) and managed care.

Traditional Health Insurance

The original type of health insurance lets you choose your own doctor. Often referred to as a *traditional indemnity* or *fee-for-service* plan, it's designed to cover big medical expenses, not every sniffle and sneeze. Most traditional indemnity plans provide two types of coverage:

• **Hospital-Surgical,** for hospital expenses and surgery performed in or out of a hospital.

• **Major Medical,** for physician services (including specialists) and drugs and medical supplies prescribed by a doctor.

There's a deductible of some sort (typically $200 for an individual and $500 for a family) that you must handle yourself before the insurance company kicks in. Once you've reached the deductible, you'll probably be required to pay about 20 percent of the bill, with the insurance company picking up the rest. (The 20 percent you pay is called the *co-payment.*) However, most plans include *stop loss provisions* that place a cap on the total you'll have to pay each year. After you've reached that cap (usually about $2,000), the insurance covers all the rest.

Make sure you understand what is covered by your company's fee-for-service offering (or any such plan you are considering buying), because policies can vary widely. In addition to hospitalization and physician services, most health insurance plans cover:

• Lab work and tests

• Prescription drugs

• Maternity care

• Annual gynecological exams

• Mammography and other screening tests

• Well-child care and immunizations

STREET SMARTS

Scott, a forty-four-year-old freelance computer programmer with a family of three, offers this advice on shopping for health insurance:

"If you're buying a policy on your own, make sure that you can renew it automatically each year without being forced to take a physical exam—just in case you develop some serious medical condition. Also, see what kind of discount you can get by raising your deductible to $1,000 or more.

"My business is doing pretty well, and my wife, son, and I are all very healthy—we typically spend less than $750 a year on doctor bills. So we raised our deductible from $1,500 to $2,500. That reduced our annual premium by about $400, which pays more than half of our yearly out-of-pocket medical expenses."

- Emergency services

- Home health care

- Transplants

- Therapy (physical, occupational, cardiac, speech, and allergy)

- Substance-abuse care

- Mental-health care

Managed-Care Insurance

You may have heard the reports some years ago about the Navy paying exorbitant prices for common household items: $404 for a socket wrench, $640 for a toilet seat, $6,000 for a simple coffeemaker. Similar outrages involving the health-care industry have been detailed on *60 Minutes* and other TV news shows—unnecessary medical treatments, procedures that were billed for but never performed, blatant overcharging, and so on. Any time the government or an insurance company is prepared to pay out money, there will be fraud.

But what happens when doctors, medical groups, and hospitals submit their bills, get paid only 80 percent (or less) of the amount, and the patient refuses to pay the other 20 percent? What happens when a dollar limit is imposed on what will be paid for a given procedure? The answer is that more procedures are performed and billed.

It was to address problems like these that insurance companies began several years ago to offer what are called *managed-care* insurance policies.

The two most common types are Health Maintenance Organization (HMO) plans and Preferred Provider Organization (PPO) plans. HMOs and PPOs supply "managed care," which really means "managed costs," because they have agreed beforehand to charge specified amounts for each treatment or procedure.

Compared to traditional indemnity (or fee-for-service) plans, managed-care policies have lower premiums. And instead of co-payments of 20 percent for most medical bills, you may be charged as little as $5 for each doctor visit, with no annual deductible.

On the downside, you'll have less choice when it comes to selecting your physician and scheduling doctor visits. Nearly all health-care providers are associated with at least one HMO or PPO. But your longtime family doctor may not belong to the same organization used by your company's health insurer, so you'll have to switch doctors if you want your visits to be covered. And if you need to see a specialist, your HMO will probably require that you first visit your primary-care physician and get a referral. (A PPO may or may not require that you get a referral.)

Coverage for the Soon-to-Be-Unemployed

If you're planning to quit your job (or even if you get fired), your first step should be to see if you can continue health-insurance coverage under your current plan. Under a federal law known as COBRA (short for Consolidated Omnibus Budget Reconcili-

SMART DEFINITION

HMO
Health Maintenance Organization. Under an HMO plan, you're required to select a primary-care physician (PCP) within the HMO network to coordinate all of your medical care. When you visit your PCP (or a specialist authorized by your PCP), your out-of-pocket cost may be as little as $5 or $10. If you use a doctor outside the plan or go to a specialist without a referral, you'll have to pay 100 percent of the bill (unless it was a true emergency situation).

Lifetime Limit
Health insurance policies often specify a *lifetime limit*—the maximum they will pay over the time you are insured. Such limits should be at least one million dollars, and preferably several million. The best policies don't impose a lifetime limit, but be sure to investigate.

ation Act of 1986), companies with at least twenty employees are required to give you that option for up to eighteen months, so be sure to ask.

You can be charged up to 102 percent of what the coverage costs (the extra 2 percent is for paperwork and handling costs), but it will almost certainly be less money than you'd pay for a comparable individual policy. And it will buy you some time to shop for the best deal on a new health-insurance plan.

You might start by contacting these companies:

• **Blue Cross and Blue Shield.** They are the largest providers of fee-for-service and managed-care policies in the United States. Check your local phone directory's yellow pages under Insurance, or visit their web site at www.bluecares.com.

• **Quotesmith Price Comparison Service.** Call 800-556-9393 or visit the Quotesmith web site at www.quotesmith.com for health-insurance quotes from one hundred companies.

• **USAA.** For auto and homeowner coverage, USAA insures only military officers, certain enlisted personnel, and other groups. But anyone can apply for life insurance and annuities. Call 800-531-8000 for more information.

Life Insurance Simplified

There are three major considerations when it comes to life insurance. First and foremost is determining whether or not you need it—not everyone does. Second is deciding what kind you should buy. And third is figuring out how much coverage you need. Unlike health insurance, life insurance isn't a necessity for everyone. For the vast majority of people, the only reason to buy life insurance is that someone depends on their income. If the kids have moved out, the college bills and mortgage are paid off, and you've accumulated enough money for your surviving spouse to live in comfort, you probably don't need life insurance. Similarly, if you are a single individual with no dependents, it rarely makes sense to buy life insurance.

Buy Term Insurance

If you need life insurance, most experts agree that the only kind of to consider is *term insurance,* either *annually renewable* or *level-premium.* Forget about cash-value policies (also known as whole life, universal life, permanent life, and other names). Term insurance is pure insurance: You pay a given premium based mainly on your age, health, and the amount of coverage you want for a certain number of years. If you die while the policy is in effect, the insurance company pays the full amount. Plain and simple—and cheap!

How Much Should You Buy?

The amount of life insurance you buy should be determined by your current and future earnings. To put it another way: Life insurance is designed to provide a lump-sum payout that will largely replace your income when you are gone.

SMART SOURCES

To find a good rate on term life insurance, try these quote services:

Quotesmith
800-556-9393
www.quotesmith.com
Maintains a database of more than 325 insurers. Offers advice and assistance by phone.

QuickQuote
702-831-2404
www.quickquote.com
Represents only thirty-five insurers, but they're all at least "A-rated" by A. M. Best.

SelectQuote
800-289-5807
www.selectquote.com
A database of eighteen companies. The web site is for information only.

Wholesale Insurance Network (WIN)
800-808-5810
A discount broker for products from eleven companies.

STREET SMARTS

If you belong to a union, professional organization, trade association, or even a college alumni club, check to see if the group offers health insurance. Such an offering proved to be just the ticket for Jackie, a thirty-eight-year-old commercial artist in a large Midwestern city who had long dreamed of fleeing the corporate world. "I knew I could make it on my own," she says, "but I had an aunt who had worked hard, saved all her life, and then got absolutely wiped out when she developed breast cancer. No health insurance. So I wasn't about to make a move until I got that solved.

"It turned out that around here, if you're in business for yourself, you can just join the Chamber of Commerce and get in on a group health-care policy. You've still got to pay, but a lot less than if you were buying a policy on your own."

That doesn't mean that if you have twenty years to retirement, the benefit has to be twenty times your current salary. Rather, it means that if your current salary is $80,000 a year, you should think in terms of insuring yourself for an amount that could gross $80,000 a year if it were invested after you're gone. The policy's death benefit thus replaces your income, assuming it is invested by your survivors. If you assume an interest rate of about 10 percent, you'd need a death benefit of about $800,000 to throw off $80,000 a year in interest.

These are very rough figures, for the point is not to provide dollar-amount advice but to get you thinking along the most productive lines. It may be that you will want to increase your coverage to include money to help with your kids' college expenses. You may want to boost it further to account for inflation, or to pay funeral costs, estate taxes, inheritance taxes, and uninsured medical costs.

But the bedrock should be this: How much money must be invested to throw off enough income to replace my salary? Add to this any other expenses you want your death benefit to pay for, and you will arrive at the amount of term-life coverage you should buy.

Getting Disability Insurance

It's a gruesome thought, but if you're an experienced machinist and lose part of your hand in an accident, if you are a sales executive and are paralyzed after a fall from a ladder while cleaning the gutters on your home, if you're a dockworker who gets his leg crushed between a cement pier and a ship's hull, you will be rendered unable to perform your normal duties. You may be unable to earn your former income—or any income at all—and thus suddenly find yourself and your family in serious financial trouble.

That's what disability insurance is for. But note this: Because their injuries occurred while they were performing their jobs, the machinist and the dockworker would probably be covered by workers' compensation, a special type of disability insurance for on-the-job accidents. But the sales executive whose accident occurred at home probably would not be covered by her employer's disability insurance plan. Only a handful of states (California, Hawaii, New Jersey, New York, and Rhode Island) currently require companies to provide coverage for injuries that occur outside of work.

Questions to Ask about Disability Insurance

Before you accept a job offer, ask about the company's disability insurance benefits. A firm may have a wonderful life insurance and health insurance package but offer little or nothing for disability coverage. That means that if, for whatever reason, you become physically or mentally unable to perform the job for which you were hired, you might be fired, with no benefits paid.

If you have to buy a policy on your own, either because you're self-employed or because your employer's plan is inadequate, the rates you'll pay are likely to be higher than those an employer would be charged for the same coverage. But if

SMART DEFINITION

Level-Premium Term Insurance

A term policy that lasts a set number of years (typically ten, fifteen, or twenty) and allows you to lock in the annual premium for the entire period. When the policy expires, you'll have to pass a medical exam to renew your coverage. Level-premium insurance is probably less expensive than annually-renewable in the long run, particularly if you're in good health and can qualify for the best rates. It's also a good choice if you're fairly confident that you'll no longer need life insurance by the time the policy expires.

you pay your own premiums, any disability income payments you receive will be tax-free. If an employer pays the premiums, in contrast, the benefits are taxable.

Here are the main points to consider:

• **What percentage of your current income will you receive if you're disabled?** Don't be surprised to find that your employer's plan, if they offer one, pays around 60 percent of your current income, up to a certain maximum—usually $5,000 to $6,000 per month—until you reach age sixty-five.

• **What's the definition of "disability"?** The distinction here is between being able to perform the work you normally do ("own occupation") and being able to do some kind of work for which you are trained after becoming disabled.

• **Guaranteed renewable/noncancelable.** If you are in poor health, and if your policy lacks this provision, the policy can be canceled when it comes up for renewal. At the very least, you will have to take a physical.

• **Lag time.** This is the period of time between when you become disabled and when you can begin collecting benefits. The longer the lag time (also referred to as a *waiting period* or *elimination period*), the lower your premiums will be.

• **COLA (cost-of-living adjustment).** A provision that automatically increases your benefit to keep pace with inflation.

Five Ways to Save Money on Term Life Insurance

1. Do your homework. If your employer provides life insurance as a benefit, great. But don't assume the coverage is adequate for your particular situation, or that buying additional insurance through your employer's group policy is necessarily the best deal. Depending on your age, health, and lifestyle, you may qualify for substantially lower rates. The easiest way to find out is to use an insurance quote service like Quotesmith or QuickQuote.

2. Quit smoking. Life insurance rates for smokers are often *double* the rates for nonsmokers. And most insurance companies make no distinction between those who smoke two packs a day or one cigar every other weekend.

3. Lose weight. Being overweight can boost your life insurance premiums by 30 percent or more. If you've lost weight since you applied for your current policy, you should definitely consider reapplying.

4. Ignore the extras. Insurance companies will try to sell you a host of extra-cost features. The *waiver of premium* option, for example, guarantees that coverage will continue if you're disabled and can't pay the premium. But why buy this if you already have sufficient disability insurance? The *accidental death* option, which provides your beneficiaries with double the face amount of the policy if you die in an accident, makes even less sense. Think about it: The chances of your dying in an accident are pretty low, and if you do, why do your survivors need twice as much money?

5. Shop around every few years. The life insurance business is very competitive. If you bought an annually-renewable term insurance policy five or six years ago, the premiums today might be double what they were the first year. By switching to a level-premium policy, you might save hundreds, if not thousands, of dollars in annual life insurance costs. Use a quote service or call your insurance agent to find out.

Congress has passed laws guaranteeing that you can continue your coverage even if you lose or quit your job. If you must purchase health insurance on your own, focus on getting coverage for major medical expenses, with a high deductible. Life insurance may *not* be essential, however. It all depends on whether you have dependents who count on your income for support. If you do, figure out how much coverage you need and shop for a low-cost term-life policy. And while you're in insurance-planning mode, make sure you understand what (if anything) your employer offers in the way of disability coverage. If you work for a living, you need disability insurance to help replace your income in case you're suddenly unable to work because of an illness or injury.

Insurance Company Ratings

Several organizations evaluate and rate companies that offer health, life, and disability insurance, assigning letter grades for overall financial strength or claims-paying ability. Trouble is, each one uses its own variation on the A-B-C grading system we're all familiar with from school. So an A+ is the top rating from Weiss Research, but at A. M. Best, the top rating is A++ (with A+ being second best). To be safe, stick with insurance companies that hold one of the top three ratings from two or three of the rating agencies listed here.

Agency	What They Rate	Top Ratings
A. M. Best	Financial Strength	A++
		A+
		A
Duff & Phelps	Claims-Paying Ability	AAA
		AA+
		AA
Moody's	Financial Strength	Aaa
		Aa1 Aa2 Aa3
		A1 A2 A3
Standard & Poor's	Claims-Paying Ability	AAA AAAq AA+
		AA AAq
Weiss Research	Safety	A+
		A
		A-

How to Think about Investing

One of the fundamental tenets of existentialism is that each individual assumes full responsibility for the consequences of his or her actions—without any certain knowledge beforehand of what's right or wrong or what's good or bad. And there's no exit from this dilemma, since even doing nothing is, in effect, making a choice.

That's a scary thought, but when you think about it, it pretty much describes the way many people feel about investing. You get a fat packet of information asking you to choose your retirement benefits. There are lots of options and lots of explanations, but no guidance on what to do.

Yet this is your retirement. It's crucial. And choosing the wrong path can make a big difference in the amount of money you'll have years down the road. *Not* making a choice is not an option. Add to this all the ads pushing various brokerage firms, investment newsletters, and a financial "products," and your head spins. As an antidote, here are some very clear, simple truths and sound advice.

Investment Basics

First, forget all the terms you may have heard for various investment products. There are only two ways to make your money grow: You either "rent it out" or you use it to buy something you think will appreciate over time. Renting money means making a loan to someone who agrees to pay you interest. Perhaps the two purest forms of renting/loaning money are putting it into a savings account or buying a CD (certificate of deposit) or some sort of bond (corporate, Treasury, municipal, or other).

Using your money to buy something, on the other hand, can mean buying a piece of a company by purchasing shares of its stock, buying real estate (a house, an apartment complex, a tract of unimproved land, etc.), or starting a small business.

Professionals use the terms *debt* securities for investments like bonds and *equity* securities for ownership investments like stocks. Those are the two options we'll consider here. The many pros and cons of investing in real estate or in a small business are beyond the scope of this book and beyond the horizon of most readers.

Risk and Return

The second major point to focus on is the difference between *stocks* (ownership) and *bonds* (lending) from an investor's perspective. In general, bonds are considered a very safe way to protect your capital while earning an acceptable return. Stocks may pay a greater return, but they carry a higher risk. That's why whenever there is economic or political uncertainty, dollars tend to fly out of stocks and into bonds, like birds flying up into the safety of the trees at the approach of a cat. When the threat departs, the money flutters back down again to enjoy the possibility of the generally higher returns offered by equities.

This is also the reason that many investment professionals recommend that you keep 60 percent of your money in stocks (for long-term growth), 30 percent in bonds (for short-term safety), and 10 percent in cash (for quick access). Those percentages can be adjusted upward or downward depending on your age, financial situation, and the amount of risk you can tolerate.

F.Y.I.

Over the past hundred years, investments in stocks have returned an average of 10 percent a year. Investments in bonds have returned about 5 percent annually. And savings accounts have averaged about 4 percent a year.

Better to Own Than to Loan

The third point to keep in mind is that owning is almost always better than loaning. That's because when you own something—like a share of stock—you participate financially in the company's success. If the company does well, you get more in stock dividends, and the price of your shares goes up. If you loan money to that same company by buying one of its bonds, the rate of interest you will earn will have absolutely nothing to do with the company's success in the marketplace.

The flip side is also true: If the company does badly and you have one of its bonds, you are virtually guaranteed to earn the specified interest rate on your investment. In fact, you'll be paid before the stockholders. But if you "own" and the company does badly, its stock price will fall and you will lose part of your investment. Fortunately, much of the time the loss will be temporary. That's because the stock prices of really good, sound companies may dip for a period, but they almost always rise again, often to even loftier heights.

Four Crucial Investment Truths

Everything said so far is so solidly supported by facts that no one disagrees with it. Buying and holding stocks over time is one of the best ways ever invented to build wealth.

So the next logical question is: What's the best way to buy stocks? Here opinions differ. And some of those opinions are not untainted with conflicts of interest. Simple solutions do exist, but hold these truths in mind as we approach them:

• **Truth 1: Stockbrokers and others make money only when you buy or sell a security.** It is thus in their financial interest to persuade you to trade frequently. "Our research indicates that XYZ Semi-conductors is about to explode. How many shares should I put you down for?" Or "The ABC company is on the short list for a big new Pentagon contract. Interested?" Think of yourself as a savvy brook trout being presented with a new fly. Do you rise to the bait or not? (And regardless of what you do, your stockbroker will keep on fishing, trying to present you with something you'll go for.)

• **Truth 2: Investing is often ego-based.** The financial arena may be about combat and victory, but it is not driven by testosterone alone. Males and females alike enjoy boasting about their investment successes and even relating their investment failures. Why? Because, win or lose, it shows that you're a "player." You're not just a manager, a lawyer, or a salesperson. You've got money to invest, and you're in charge. You've got sources, you've got a system, you're smarter than most. At a cocktail party, if you can't talk sports, talk investments!

• **Truth 3: Hot tips and claims of inside information are usually yesterday's news.** "A friend of a friend who is the manicurist for the wife of the CEO of MegaCorp said to buy Whimpy-Blimpy, P.L.C., right now. Big developments are on the way." Unfortunately, unless you work at a high level in the industry, by the time you or anyone you know has gotten an accurate hot tip, it's history. Leaving aside the laws against insider trad-

SMART MONEY

The key to building truly serious wealth is to discipline yourself to regularly invest in quality stocks and to hold on to them over time. In a recent edition of his newsletter *Louis Rukeyser's Wall Street,* Mr. Rukeyser recounts the story of Anne Scheiber, an amateur investor who put $5,000 into a few quality stocks in 1944. "She almost *never* traded," says Mr. Rukeyser. "When she died in 1995, her $5,000 had turned into $22 million—a rate of return that places her in the company of superstar investor Warren Buffett."

SMART SOURCES

All publicly held companies—firms that sell their stock to the public—are required to present the complete details of their operations to the Securities and Exchange Commission (SEC). These filings are public information, easily obtainable by mail. Call 800-732-0330 for information or contact the Internet site at www.edgar.com.

ing, ask yourself this: Why would anybody who *really* knew something share it with anyone else?

• **Truth 4: There is a huge and highly profitable industry devoted to selling you advice on which stocks to buy, sell, or hold.** The notion is that you have a job to do and a life to live, so there's no way you can spend the time needed to collect, sift, and act upon all the information you need to make wise investment decisions. And besides, as a member of the public, you really don't have access to the plant tours, executive briefings, and other kinds of information companies provide to the research departments of major brokerage firms. In point of fact, anyone with access to a good library or an Internet connection can nearly duplicate the information provided to research department professionals.

Buying Stocks and Mutual Funds

The two main ways to buy stocks are to either do it yourself or to hire someone else to do it for you, usually by purchasing shares in a stock mutual fund. Let's take a look at the pros and cons of each approach.

Mutual Funds: Pros

• You don't have to come up with investment ideas, do the research on companies, and decide which stocks to buy or sell.

• You don't have to constantly monitor the performance of the stocks you own.

• By their very nature, mutual funds are diversified (most funds typically hold about 120 different stocks). So, when some of the stocks are down, some will probably be up. Indeed, using diversification to smooth out an investor's ride was the main reason mutual funds were created in the first place.

• There are more than 5,000 stock mutual funds to choose from, each with a different focus or investment philosophy. Some funds concentrate on blue-chip companies, for example. Others zero in on a particular economic sector. More than likely, you can find a fund that matches your goals.

• You can get into many funds with an investment of $1,000 or less. In contrast, it usually doesn't make sense to buy less than $5,000 to $10,000 of a stock in a single purchase, due to the transaction fees you'll pay, even to a discount broker.

Mutual Funds: Cons

• **Fees.** Some funds force you to pay a sales commission, called a *load,* at some point in the process—when you buy in (A shares), sell out (B shares), or annually (C shares). The load can be as low as 2 percent and as high as 8.5 percent of the amount you invest. *No-load* funds don't have such charges, but like all funds, they assess annual management and administrative fees (typically about 1.41 percent), and charge you for your share of the transaction fees the fund pays when it

"I should have paid *more* attention," says David, an internist in Glendale, California. "I bought no-load funds. But I got my statement and there was a 12b-1 fee that amounted to a quarter of a percent.

"Then I learned that the SEC's regulation 12b-1 lets funds charge for advertising, marketing, and distribution. And they can charge it every year! I got out of that fund fast, but you've got to watch them every minute." Most no-load funds don't charge for 12b-1 expenses, even though they are permitted to, up to a maximum of 0.25 percent. Load funds can charge up to 1.25 percent a year.

The key thing is to *check the prospectus!* Don't sign up for anything or send any fund any money until you have read and understand all the fees laid out in the prospectus.

trades stocks (about 1.39 percent). Add up these two figures, and you're paying a total of about 2.8 percent a year to have someone else pick the stocks and do the investing.

• **Performance.** According to *Consumer Reports,* "Of the 2,029 domestic equity funds that have competed for investors' dollars since 1995, fewer than six percent have matched or beaten the returns of the Standard & Poor's 500." *Money* magazine adds that, largely because of the "expense hurdle" of management fees, over periods of a decade or more, 80 percent of U.S. diversified stock funds underperform the S&P 500. (The Dow Jones Industrial Average tracks thirty blue-chip stocks, but the Standard & Poor's 500 tracks five hundred stocks, and thus offers a broader picture of the performance of the stock market as a whole.)

• **Taxes.** Whenever you make money on an investment, you will owe taxes once you realize your gains by selling it. Because stock profits are capital gains, and because of the twists of the capital-gains law, the amount you owe will depend on how long the fund has held the stock. The percentage owed to Uncle Sam can range from the rate you pay on ordinary income (39.6 percent at the top), to 28 percent if the stock has been held for more than a year but less than 18 months, to 20 percent if the stock has been held for eighteen months or longer. (The required holding period to qualify for the 20 percent rate may have been reduced to 12 months as you read this.) The key point is that you have no control over when the fund manager chooses to realize gains and thus no control over when and how much you will owe in capital-gains taxes.

Picking Stocks: Pros

• **The possibility of higher returns.** If you know the companies and products in your own field, you probably have some opinions on which ones would make good investments. And that can give you the edge you need to outperform the S&P 500.

• **There are no management fees or sales loads.** But there are brokerage commissions whenever you buy or sell a stock. These can be minimized by using a discount broker (or even buying stock directly from the company) and by following a "buy-and-hold" approach.

• **You have the freedom to create a well-balanced portfolio** that suits your personal desires, goals, and needs.

• **You are in complete control of when you take a capital gain,** so to a large extent you can determine the rate of the capital-gains tax you will pay.

• **Tools exist on the Internet and on CD-ROM that make it relatively easy to screen for stocks** meeting your criteria, putting you on a nearly equal footing with a fund manager when it comes to getting information about a company or an industry.

Picking Stocks: Cons

• **Trading costs.** The average price of a stock on the New York Stock Exchange is $43. If you buy one hundred shares at $43 each from a discount

F.Y.I.

There *are* mutual funds that focus on reducing tax liability, but let's not cloud the picture right now, other than to say that it is not a good idea to buy into a fund at the end of the year, since that's when most pay out capital-gains distributions to shareholders. If you buy shares in a fund right before it distributes its capital gains, you will owe capital-gains taxes even though you yourself have not seen any rise in the value of your investment.

F.Y.I.

Many investor newsletters and gurus use the bid (or last-trade) price when calculating the performance of the stocks they've recommended in the past. This is sheer fantasy, since no one can buy the stock at the bid price. Some investment publishers fail to include stockbroker commissions as well when calculating returns. So watch out!

broker, you will be charged between $30 and $55. That's over 1 percent of your $4,300 investment. Depending on the number of shares and the amount of money you're investing, brokerage commissions can range from 1 to 4 percent. A commission will also be deducted when you sell, further reducing your effective return.

• **The spread.** All stocks have two prices: the price you pay when you buy (the *ask* price) and the price a brokerage will pay you when you sell it (the *bid* price). It's the bid price that you see in the newspapers and on stock tickers as the "last trade." The spread compensates the brokerage and other "market makers" for holding inventories of stocks and matching buyers and sellers. Spreads range from a half percent to 6 percent.

• **Time and effort.** Doing the research needed to pick stocks, and then monitoring their performance, can be a full-time job. At the very least, it will require time and energy that could be spent with your family or simply having fun.

• **The difficulty of outperforming the market.** According to *Louis Rukeyser's Mutual Funds* newsletter, 93 percent of stock-fund managers—people who analyze and pick stocks—fail to beat the S&P 500 each year. You might be able to do so owning only a handful of high-flying stocks, but that can be the equivalent of putting all your eggs in one basket. You won't have the volatility-damping benefits of diversity. And should you opt for diversity, your portfolio's performance will almost certainly be reduced, since the whole point of diversifying is that when one stock is down another is up.

What's the Right Approach?

There's no reason why you can't buy mutual funds and also buy stocks on your own. And it doesn't have to be a big deal. According to *Money* magazine, fund investors typically own just three funds and stock investors typically hold just three stocks. However, before you begin any investment program, you might want to consider taking the following steps:

• **Step 1: Fully fund your IRA, Keogh, 401(k), and other plans that let you use pre-tax dollars to earn tax-deferred interest.** If you're in your twenties or thirties, this should be your absolute number-one priority. By being an "early investor," you'll reap the benefits of long-term, tax-deferred compounding.

• **Step 2: Resolve to stay away from any kind of investment that you don't completely understand.** This includes puts and calls (options trading), short selling, warrants, limited partnerships, zero-coupon bonds, or any of the other exotica Wall Street comes up with. In particular, resolve to stay far, far away from commodities (futures in orange juice, home-heating oil, pork bellies, and the like).

How to Buy Stocks Commission-Free

Tired of seeing brokerage commissions and ask-price percentages eating into your return? Well, you may be able to cut out the middleman and buy directly from the company. More than a thousand firms allow you to set up Direct Stock-Purchase (DSP), Direct Purchase Programs (DPP), or Dividend Reinvestment Programs (DRIP). Most plans are structured to encourage long-term ownership, which is usually a good idea. And many let you invest as little as $25 to $50 at a time. A few small transaction fees ($5 or so) may be involved, but the only real drawback is that selling the stock involves a few more steps than simply calling your broker.

For more information, consult the *Directory of Dividend Reinvestment Plans*, available for $16 from NorthStar Financial (800-233-5922). On the Web, you can visit Netstock Direct at www.netstockdirect.com, or visit the Society for Direct Investing at www.sdinews.org.

SMART MONEY

Commenting on the dangers of commodities trading, Andrew Tobias had this to say in his famous book *The Only Investment Guide You'll Ever Need*: "It is a fact that 90 percent or more of the people who play the commodities game get burned. I submit that you have now read all you need ever read about commodities."

• **Step 3: Figure out how much money you can afford to invest each month. Then do it!** Month after month, year after year. There will always be some home improvement or car repair or other expense you can use as an excuse for skipping a month. But don't. Be relentless.

• **Step 4: Use your initial contributions to pay off your credit cards.** If you're being charged 18 percent (or worse) a year on your balance, you can effectively "earn" that return each time you pay off a dollar of the principal. Get the cards paid down, then cancel them or lock them away and use a debit card instead.

• **Step 5: Take the long view.** The stock market may have gone up, up, and up for a decade or more, but that doesn't mean it won't ever go down and stay down for an extended period of time. Over the long term, a bear market of a year or more doesn't really matter. If you've bought a quality stock or mutual fund, it will eventually go back up. Investments in stock are for long-term gains. Buy the good stuff, hold on to it, and don't worry about down markets.

• **Step 6: Diversify!** The fact that the stock market always rises over time is cold comfort if all your money is tied up in stocks and you need to make a down payment on a house. You'll have to sell stock and give up the gains you would have made when the market rebounds. That's why it's a good idea to keep some of your money in debt securities. When the stock market is down, the bond market is usually up. And, in any case, if you own quality bonds or bond mutual funds, your principal will be safe while it earns an acceptable rate of return.

The traditional distribution of 60 percent in stocks, 30 percent in bonds, and 10 percent in cash is a good starting point. But if you've paid off your credit cards, you could use them as "cash" in an emergency. And in a bull market, you might want to put more into stocks and less into a savings account, money market, or other cash equivalents.

• **Step 7: Don't get greedy.** It's human nature to want the highest possible return on your money. That's why otherwise intelligent people who would never doubt, say, the law of gravity deny the existence of equally powerful and demonstrable economic laws, such as the fact that there is no exceptionally high reward without exceptionally high risk. And this assumes criminal behavior is not involved. If you're dealing with a crook, you're guaranteed to lose everything.

Dollar-Cost Averaging

The best way to invest is to, in fact, *invest,* and to do so on a regular basis. It sounds simpleminded, but it's not. It takes discipline to invest even $100 every month, month in and month out, no matter what. But it really is the key to financial security. And it provides a very important benefit you may not know about: It lets you harness the power of *dollar-cost averaging.*

Dollar-cost averaging frees you from the need to closely monitor the market and the stocks you own to determine (or rather, guess at) just the right moment to buy. By regularly investing the same amount in the same high-quality security month after month, you will acquire fewer shares

SMART DEFINITIONS

Bull Market
A period of rising stock-market prices, when market optimists (the bulls) drive up the cost of buying stocks.

Bear Market
A falling market, with stock prices dropping 15 percent or more. Historically, the stock market has tended to rise more than it falls. Since 1960, there have been only six bear markets.

SMART SOURCES

The following magazine issues all offer "best-buy" mutual fund lists at some point during the year:

• *Forbes.* Second August issue and first February issue.

• *Business Week.* Starting with the third week in January, and continuing for three consecutive weeks.

• *Money.* February and August issues.

• *Kiplinger's Personal Finance Magazine.* August or September issue. A separate mutual funds issue is published each February.

when the price is high, but you'll buy more shares when the price is low.

For example, suppose you invest $100 a month in a favorite mutual fund. In the first month, shares are $10, so your $100 buys ten shares. The next month, the shares are $20, so you get five shares. You now own fifteen shares, and you have invested $200. Your average cost per share is $13.33. On the other hand, if you had decided that you were going to buy a certain number of shares instead of investing a certain amount of money and had bought ten shares at $10 and ten shares at $20, you would have invested $300, you would own twenty shares, and your average cost per share would be $15.

Certainly the ideal would have been to have bought twenty or thirty shares at $10 each and then watch the price rise to $20 a share. But how can you expect to be that prescient when even the pros can't consistently beat the market?

Index Funds

As noted earlier, investing is not free of ego and emotion. To some, it is a combat sport. Nothing wrong with that, as long as the money you're "playing with" is not your nest egg. Considering that fewer than 10 percent of mutual fund managers beat the market in any given year, and virtually no one beats the market year in and year out, it simply makes good sense to "buy the market."

That's what *index funds* do. Most are run by a computer that has been assigned the task of replicating a given market index, like the Standard & Poor's 500. Because the computer takes no salary, operating expenses are typically a full percentage point below the typical fund managed by a Harvard MBA. And while you're not likely to do much better than the market, you're sure not going to do much worse. There is also the fact that such funds do much less trading, so there are fewer taxable distributions. No, it's not exciting or thrilling, but over a period of ten years or more, an index fund typically outperforms 75 percent of its non-index competitors. That's why buying shares in an "index fund" that mindlessly (and fee-lessly) tracks the S&P 500 is often a pretty good idea.

The Vanguard Group is the largest provider of index mutual funds, so you may want to start by examining its offerings. (For information, contact 800-662-7447; on the Web, at www.vanguard.com.) Many other companies offer similar products.

Information on Funds

Far more information about mutual funds is available than any single individual can absorb. And not all of it is relevant or even accurate. Fortunately, there are a few generally reliable, easily understood sources you can turn to.

One of the best is *Morningstar Mutual Funds,* a monthly print publication that you might find at your local library. (To order, call 800-735-0700 and ask about their $55 three-month trial offer.) *Morningstar* is also available on the Internet (www.morningstar.net) and on America Online (Keyword: Morningstar), where you can look at list of the top twenty-five mutual funds, the top twenty-five foreign stock funds, and more.

SMART DEFINITION

Index

Some people are surprised to learn that the famous Dow Jones Industrial Average is an index comprising the shares of just thirty U.S. companies. Some would say that thirty stocks is a pretty thin sample. That's why McGraw-Hill's subsidiary, Standard & Poor's, compiled an index of five hundred of the most widely held common stocks, which represent 80 percent of the market value of the entire New York Stock Exchange. This is the "S&P 500," and it is generally considered the best measure of overall market growth.

The S&P 500 index is the yardstick. If you or your mutual fund managers can beat it, you're doing very well. But, after all costs are deducted from the bottom line, the majority of mutual funds will lose to the S&P 500 year after year.

THE BOTTOM LINE

The most important thing about investing is to do it and do it now! When it comes to compounding, time really is money, so the sooner you start, the more money you will have in the end. Start by fully funding any tax-deferred options available to you. Then decide on a sum and invest it regularly each month, month in and month out.

For many people, an index mutual fund offers the most convenient and inexpensive way to make sure that returns match those of the market as a whole. There's tons of information available to help you make your investing decisions—magazines, books, online sources. Or, as you'll learn in the next chapter, you can hire a fee-based (not commission-compensated) financial adviser to help you draw up a sound plan.

Information on Stocks

Because they are managing their own portfolios, do-it-yourself stock investors need more information and assistance than mutual fund buyers. So even more information is available. A good place to start is with a subscription to the *Wall Street Journal*. Then add a subscription to either *Business Week, Barron's,* or *Forbes. Money, SmartMoney,* and *Kiplinger's Personal Finance Magazine* are also good choices, since the goal here is to get a broad overview.

To zero in on specific stocks, go to your library and look for the weekly issue of the *Value Line Investment Survey.* You can also buy it, of course, but it's expensive—$570 for an annual print subscription. (It's also available as a monthly Windows-compatible CD-ROM for $595.) For more information, call 800-833-0046 or visit the company's web site at www.valueline.com.

For more background in stock investing, read the classic books on the subject, including these titles:

• *The Intelligent Investor* by Benjamin Graham (HarperCollins, 1997).

• *The Battle for Investment Survival* by Gerald M. Loeb (John Wiley, 1996).

• *Stock Market Primer* by Claude N. Rosenberg, Jr. (Warner Books, 1991).

Saving for College and Retire- ment

Financial independence, which most of us define as being able to live a comfortable life without having to work, is probably everyone's most cherished investment goal. Certainly that's what saving for retirement is all about. And yet most people have no idea how to figure out how much money they'll need to support themselves in retirement, or where the money will come from. The other goal most people save for is to fund their children's college education.

These are two excellent goals. The trouble is that if you don't pay attention to how the system works in each case, you won't maximize your investments. Let's start with college.

Treating College Like a Major Purchase

Studies have shown that over their working lives, college graduates earn substantially more than those with just a high school or community college diploma. That's the reality of the marketplace.

But there are other realities. According to the College Board, when you take into consideration tuition, room and board, books, activity fees, and some transportation expenses, the average annual cost of attending a four-year college or university for the 1996–97 school year was $10,100 for public or state institutions and $21,400 for private schools.

A private education, in other words, is more than double the price of going to a state university. But how many parents—even those who would bargain a car dealer down to within an inch of his life—fail to ask the simple question: Is it worth it? Does a degree from a private college give you twice the value? What does your child get for the *extra* $45,200 you might spend over those four years?

No book can answer these questions, although if you've been to college yourself, you know that a college education can be as much about making future business contacts and finding a mate as it is about preparing for a job or imbibing the world's cultural traditions. The important thing is for you—and your child—to ask these questions. After all, next to buying a home, a college education is likely to be the single biggest expenditure in your life.

Paying for College

Here are some suggestions and tips from insiders that will help you understand the financial-aid game and get you started in the right direction toward finding a way to pay those college bills:

Tip 1: Start planning as soon as your child is born. You won't have to face the expense for another eighteen years, but there are steps, like setting up special tax-deferred accounts, that can pay big benefits in the future. An excellent book to consult is *Making the Most of Your Money* by Jane Bryant Quinn (Simon & Schuster, 1997).

Tip 2: Contribute the maximum to any retirement plan that can be funded with pre-tax dollars. At this writing, the formulas used by most colleges for calculating financial aid don't count the assets

SMART MONEY

Walecia Konrad, a columnist for *Smart-Money* magazine, warns parents of these two classic mistakes when planning children's educations:

1. Putting college savings ahead of retirement savings.

"When figuring aid eligibility, schools don't consider money placed in IRS-sanctioned retirement savings accounts part of your overall assets. You may find that if you rob your retirement now to pay for your children's education, they'll have to support you when you hit sixty-five—a situation no parent relishes."

2. Assuming you won't qualify for financial aid.

"Last year close to $47 billion in aid was awarded to families of all income levels. Nearly 50 percent of all students receive at least a partial award."

SMART SOURCES

Your library or book-store is sure to have directories devoted to financial-aid sources. The best are updated regularly, so be sure to check the copyright date. Here are two good ones:

The Complete Scholarship Book by Student Services, Inc. This book lives up to its title, presenting more than five thousand scholarships, including college-specific awards not found in most other books. Published by Sourcebooks (800-432-7444). $22.95

College Money Handbook. One of several comprehensive guides to financial aid, published by Peterson's and updated every year. Includes a CD-ROM to help you explore options and estimate college costs (800-338-3282; on the Web, www.petersons.com). $26.95

in your retirement accounts. In a pinch, you might be able to tap into your retirement money. (If you have a 401(k) plan, for example, you may be able to borrow up to $50,000 and pay it back over as many as thirty years with a very attractive interest rate.) Of course, you'll want to avoid borrowing from your retirement money to pay for college if you can, since taking money out considerably reduces compounding. A better move might be to borrow against your house with a home-equity loan or second mortgage.

Tip 3: Set up an Education IRA (EdIRA) for each child as soon as possible. Up to $500 a year can be contributed to an EdIRA for anyone under age eighteen. That may not sound like much, but assuming the stock market's average return of 10 percent, by the time your child is eighteen, the account will be worth nearly $22,800, all of which can be withdrawn penalty- and tax-free if it's used for college. There are income eligibility requirements, but if you don't qualify, grandparents, godparents, and friends can make the $500 contribution.

Tip 4: Do *not* set up a custodial account in your child's name. Unless you are absolutely certain you will not qualify for financial aid, "putting money in the child's name is crazy," says Kalman Chany, author of *The Princeton Review Student Advantage Guide to Paying for College.* That's because under the federal financial-aid formula many colleges use, children are expected to put 35 percent of their savings toward college costs. The more savings they have, the less aid you'll get.

Tip 5: Negotiate! According to Frank Resnick, a former financial aid officer at Central Connecticut State University and now the school's controller, "Negotiating happens far more often than financial-aid administrators would want you to know." One technique: Play two or more colleges off against each other. Colleges will compete for desirable students. So if your child's second choice makes a better offer than the first choice, call the financial-aid officer at the first choice and ask if the school can do any better.

Tip 6: Plan your expenditures and investment activities with financial aid in mind. Your adjusted gross income (AGI) as shown on your tax forms is by far the most important factor in determining your eligibility for financial aid. But because most schools look at only the previous year's finances when your child is applying for financial aid, you can reduce what you show if you plan things properly. (Some private schools examine two years of returns.)

For example, if you take capital gains in the years when your child is applying for financial aid, the college will assume that you earn that income every year. So don't do it. Similarly, if you've been saving for a new car or for some other major expense, consider spending the money and thus removing it from your assets column.

Tip 7: Apply early and don't give up. Colleges have a pool of money each year that they can use for financial aid, and when it's gone, it's gone. So don't delay. Apply for aid at the earliest possible date. Also, don't assume that you make too much money to qualify for any form of assistance.

You or your child will almost certainly qualify for some kind of low-interest, deferred-payment loan backed by the government. This is a good deal, and only after you have maxed it out should you consider getting a second mortgage or home-equity loan.

Education Tax Credits

The 1997 budget agreement between Congress and the White House introduced two important college-expense-related tax credits that took effect in 1998—Hope Scholarships and the Lifetime Learning Credit. Here are the details.

The Hope Scholarship allows you to deduct from your tax bill 100 percent of the first $1,000 you pay in tuition and fees and 50 percent of the next $1,000, for a total tax credit of $1,500. You can take a Hope credit for each student in the family, regardless of the person's age. But the tax credit applies only during the first two years in school, whether they are spent at a community college or at a four-year institution.

The Lifetime Learning Credit can be used along with the Hope Credit. You get a credit of up to $1,000 (20 percent of the first $5,000 paid in tuition and fees) from 1998 through 2002. Beginning in 2003, you get up to $2,000 (20 percent of the first $10,000 paid in tuition and fees). The credit is available even for courses you or your spouse might take to improve job skills or as part of a continuing-education program. But your family is permitted to take only one Lifetime Credit per tax year, regardless of the number of students in the family.

"Some Restrictions Apply"

Naturally, there are a few strings attached to these generous credits, including the following:

• Neither credit can be taken in a year when you use funds kept in an EdIRA.

• If you're single, you get the full credit if your adjusted gross income (AGI) is under $40,000. Then it starts to shrink until it disappears completely at $50,000 AGI. Married couples get full credit up to $80,000, but it fades out completely at $100,000.

• You can't use both credits for the same child, but you can use one for one child and one for another. (Don't you just love tax law?) As always, you will want to check with your accountant or tax adviser before deciding what to do.

Ah, Sweet Retirement!

Next to college, the other major savings goal for most people is a comfortable retirement. But how much will you need to be comfortable? There's no easy answer to that question. Will your mortgage, college bills, and other major debts all be paid off? Are you going to continue living in the same part of the country or move someplace less expensive? Will you continue working part-time? Are you counting on Social Security for some portion of your income?

The fact is, you'll probably need more money than you think once you retire—possibly as much as 70 percent (or more) of your pre-retirement

"My father worked for the same company for almost forty years. He retired when he was sixty-three, after the doctors told him he'd have to slow down because of a mild heart attack. I was determined not to live my life that way," says Joel, an editor for a West Coast computer-book publisher.

"So we both began making regular contributions to our 401(k) plans. It's amazing how those early contributions have grown.

"We also learned to use a couple of different retirement-planning calculators—my wife likes the one that comes with Quicken, and I use a little program that I got from my company's benefits department. Once you get the hang of it, it's not all that difficult to plug in the numbers and get a rough idea of how much we'll have and what we'll need to live on without our paychecks."

income, according to a recent *Money* magazine survey of current retirees. So if you're accustomed to living on, say, $75,000 a year, you might need in the neighborhood of $52,500 a year after you retire. To generate that amount of income from your retirement savings alone, you'd need a nest egg of $525,000 earning 10 percent a year, or, figuring more conservatively, $750,000 earning 7 percent.

There are various tax and legal complexities, of course, but in the end, the key to a comfortable retirement is to start putting as many pre-tax dollars as you possibly can, as early as you can, into a tax-deferred retirement account and to continue the process through your working life. Invest the money in quality mutual funds, make contributions every year (possibly through automatic payroll deductions), and you'll probably be just fine. Ideally, when you retire at age sixty-five or so, you'll have a pension, Social Security, and your retirement savings to draw upon.

Tax-Deferred Savings!

Lots of options exist, depending on your employment status, but there is no great mystery to the process. Whether you're self-employed or work for a company, search out all the options that let you invest pre-tax dollars in accounts with earnings that are tax-deferred. Then load 'em up! And do so as soon as possible.

For example, assume you're in the 28 percent tax bracket and you've just received a $3,000 raise. If you opt to put that $3,000 into a tax-deferred retirement account, you'll be investing $3,000. But if you opt instead to be *paid* that sum, the tax will be deducted, and you will have only $2,160 to invest. And the income you earn from that $2,160 investment will be taxed every year as regular income, whereas the income earned in the tax-deferred account gets added to the principal and builds and builds and builds.

The Early-Saver Advantage

Another powerful consideration is *when* you start your investment program. If you were to begin at age twenty-five depositing $3,000 a year in a tax-deferred account, in fifteen years when you turn forty, you would have close to $84,000, assuming an average annual interest rate of 7 percent. If you then *stopped* contributing but let your investment continue to grow, by the time you turn sixty-five, you would have almost $456,000. (And keep in mind that what you paid in was $45,000— $3,000 for fifteen years.)

If, on the other hand, you were to wait until your fortieth birthday to start socking away that $3,000 a year, and then began religiously contributing that amount year after year until age sixty-five, you'd have somewhere in the neighborhood of $206,000 (again assuming a 7 percent interest rate). That's $250,000 less than if you had taken the early-saver approach. And you will have contributed substantially more—$75,000 compared to the early saver's $45,000.

The results are dramatic, but this is a rather conservative calculation. You might be able to earn the stock market's historical average of about 10 percent. And even if you were to begin your investment program early, you would probably continue to contribute after the fifteen-year mark. The point is that contributing the maximum

F.Y.I.

The latest Retirement Confidence Survey, conducted annually by the Washington-based Employee Benefit Research Institute, found that 36 percent of people questioned haven't even tried to calculate what they'll need for retirement. Close to 40 percent said that they simply didn't have the time to do the figures. Other reasons given were that they were afraid of the answers (29 percent) and that they thought the calculations would be too difficult (20 percent). For more information about the survey, call EBRI (202-659-0670) or visit their web site (www.ebri.org).

SMART SOURCES

For assistance in locating a financial planner, contact one or both of these organizations:

American Institute of Certified Public Accountants
Personal Planning Division
1211 Sixth Avenue
New York, NY 10036
800-862-4272
Ask for Product Code G00616, a free list of Personal Financial Specialists.

National Association of Personal Financial Planners (NAPFA)
355 West Dundee Road
Suite 200
Buffalo Grove, IL 60089
888-333-6659
www.napfa.org
Call the toll-free number or visit the NAPFA web site and complete the online form.

amount possible to tax-deferred plans as soon as possible can pay huge dividends later on.

The Options That Exist

If you work for a corporation, make an appointment with the benefits specialist in the human resources department. If you work for yourself, consult with your CPA or tax specialist.

There are Individual Retirement Accounts (IRAs), Roth IRAs (which are funded with after-tax dollars), 401(k) plans and their 403(b) cousins for nonprofits or state and municipal workers, SEPs (Simplified Employee Pension Plans), Keogh Plans, and more. Books and web sites like those recommended in this chapter can alert you to the questions to ask and to the ins and outs.

But ask yourself this question: No one expects me to enter a court of law without a lawyer, so why should I or anyone else expect me to deal with complex financial matters like saving for college or retirement without an adviser?

Finding a Financial Adviser

Take money, ego, and greed, and mix them with complexity, taxes, and salespeople working on commission, then drive the mixture with the piston of passing time and the undeniable need to save and invest for college and retirement, and you have a highly explosive concoction.

You work hard for your money. You want to be

able to send your child to a good college without having to live on beans and table scraps for four years. You want a comfortable retirement. But investing isn't your area of expertise, even though, judging from *Wall Street Week* on PBS, *Money* and *Worth* magazines, and radio programs like Bob Potter's *Sound Money* on NPR, a heck of a lot of people apparently not only have money but are managing their own investments. Are you missing something?

No, you are not. There are lots of people for whom investing is a sport or a form of recreation. They are not interested in "boring" index funds or in the time-tested wealth-building approach of buying quality investments and holding on to them for a long time. They crave the excitement and action of being players. Fine. Let them play, and let the various forms of the financial press feed their need. You're smarter than that.

Where to Get Professional Help When You Need It

That's not to say that you won't ever need some professional guidance. The problem is to find an adviser who will not try to sell you something. Sad to say, some stockbrokers and life insurance salespeople do a very good business masquerading as financial planners.

Just when you think you've found someone who can guide you through the complexities, they begin to recommend that you put money into a high-load mutual fund or a cash-value life insurance policy. The financial woods are dark and deep, and the wolves who live there rarely look like wolves at all. But they will strip your financial

SMART SOURCES

You can access some excellent interactive worksheets and planning kits on the Web or order them by phone. Here are some particularly good ones:

SmartMoney
Retirement Strategy Worksheets
www.smartmoney.com/ac/retirement

T. Rowe Price
Retirement Planning Worksheet
www.troweprice.com/retirement

Retirement Planning Kit
800-638-5660

Retirement Planning Analyzer Software ($19.95)
800-333-0740

Vanguard Group
Retirement Resource Center
www.vanguard.com

Vanguard Guide to Planning for Retirement ($13)
800-950-1971

College and retirement planning? Who has the time? There simply aren't enough hours in the day. But if one of your kids breaks an arm at soccer practice, you will find the time to rendezvous at the hospital emergency room. It's melodramatic, perhaps, but finding the time to plan for that same child's college education and for your own retirement is just as important an emergency. Muscles and bones will heal, but every year—every month—you put off addressing these financial issues hurts you irrevocably. When it comes to investments and the future, *time* is the crucial element. Every month you delay is a month's interest or return that you can never recover. So use the advice and the pointers in this chapter to start today.

flesh as efficiently as the wildest beast—and you won't even feel it until it's too late.

So what can you do? If you have a CPA or tax accountant, start there. Explain your needs and ask for recommendations. If you need help in locating a CPA, contact the American Institute of Certified Public Accountants for a free list of CPAs who have taken the courses necessary to become a Personal Financial Specialist (PFS). Most PFSs operate on a fee-only basis, but some earn commissions on the products they sell, so be sure to ask.

Another option to consider is contacting the National Association of Personal Financial Planners (NAPFA) for the name of a member near you. All members work on a fee-only basis. They have no financial interest in the products they recommend.

Finally, keep your common sense and natural skepticism in fighting trim. Your chances of making a killing in any legal investment are worse than your chances of winning the lottery. The difference is that when you play the lottery, you only throw away a few dollars at a time. When you fall for some perfectly legal investment scheme, with its razzle-dazzle promises of incredible future riches, you might be throwing away tens of thousands of hard-earned dollars. And that hurts.

CHAPTER 10

Taxes: How to Cope

THE KEYS

• The complexity of the tax code is no accident, and it isn't likely to change.

• Understanding your marginal tax rate (or tax bracket) will help you make financial decisions.

• Watch out for the marriage penalty. If you're married and you both work, you'll pay more in income tax than if you were single.

• Exemptions are important, but deductions are the key to it all.

• Get help! The tax code is so complex and ever changing that it's virtually impossible to master it on a part-time basis.

It happens to everyone. You get a job. The salary sounds great. And you start planning how you're going to spend your first paycheck. But when payday arrives, you look at how small the check is and say, "There must be some mistake. I don't believe it. Did you see how much they took out?" For many of us, this moment marks the real transition from childhood to adulthood, for paying taxes is an ever-present part of grown-up life.

Why *Should* the Tax Code Make Any Sense?

You don't have to be in the work force long before you begin to realize that the real world doesn't work the way your junior-high civics teacher said it did. Despite their public pronouncements, for example, politicians of all parties like to spend money. And their constituents reelect them for doing so as long as the pork, as it's called, is spent in their districts or states.

There's nothing inherently wrong with this. Roads have to be built and maintained. We need some kind of national defense. And certainly, in this country of plenty, no one should go hungry. The problems—and the tax code complexities— begin when trade associations, unions, individual companies, and others lobby Congress for exemptions and other special treatment. The complexities are compounded when politicians try to use the tax code as an instrument of public policy to encourage one kind of behavior and discourage another. This is why Congress keeps changing things and why most experts agree that the tax code itself doesn't make much sense.

Marginal and Effective Tax Rates

The United States uses what's called a *progressive* income tax system. That doesn't mean that it's modern, forward-thinking, and up to date. The term refers to the fact that the tax rates move progressively higher as a person's income increases. At this writing, there are five tax rates, ranging from 15 percent to 39.6 percent. Ask most people what percentage of their income they pay in federal income taxes and a good many of them will probably respond with one of those rates. And most will be wrong.

The reason they're wrong is that they are confusing the *marginal* tax rate (also referred to as the *tax bracket*) and the *effective* tax rate. Because your pay stub shows the same amount being withheld from each paycheck, you probably are not aware that the income you earn earlier in the year is actually taxed at a lower rate than the last dollar you earn.

For example, suppose you're single and your total taxable income is $80,000 a year. You'll pay 15 percent on the first $25,350 you earn. But on the next $36,050 you earn, you'll pay 28 percent. And as your year's total approaches the full amount, you'll pay 31 percent on the final $18,600 you earn.

In this case, the percentage of your income paid in federal income taxes (your effective tax rate) will be about 23 percent. Your marginal tax

F.Y.I.

If it seems that more and more of your hard-earned money goes to paying taxes year after year, you're probably right. In 1970, the average American household worked from January 1 through April 26 to pay federal, state, and local taxes. In 1980, Tax Freedom Day, a term coined by the Washington-based Tax Foundation (www.taxfoundation.org), was May 1. By 1990, it had moved by just a single day to May 2, indicating that taxes had not risen much during the decade. But in 1997, Tax Freedom Day was celebrated on May 9.

The Marriage Penalty

It's estimated that some 21 million Americans are affected by what is known as the *marriage penalty.* This means that two people who are married end up paying an average of $1,400 more in federal income tax than they would earning the same incomes and simply living together. The marriage penalty can be significant if you and your spouse earn identical incomes. But it's even worse when one spouse earns substantially more than the other.

That's because, when determining the tax bracket, the law treats a family's income as if it had been earned by one individual. Let's say, for example, that your taxable income is $80,000, which puts you in the 28 percent tax bracket. Your spouse takes a part-time job that pays $20,000—the same job that was taxed at 15 percent the year before you were married. Your total taxable income is now $100,000, which means that your spouse's income will be taxed not at 15 percent but at 28 percent.

Even worse are situations in which a spouse's income pushes your family into a higher tax bracket than you'd be in with just your salary. In addition, popular exemptions and tax credits start to be phased out once your total income reaches a certain level. Fortunately, a Marriage Tax Elimination Act has been introduced in the House of Representatives. So as you read this, it may be history.

rate (or tax bracket), on the other hand, will indeed be 31 percent.

So why does it matter? It matters because the marginal tax rate is the rate applied to the last dollar you earn. Being aware of your marginal tax rate/tax bracket helps you evaluate all kinds of financial decisions. How much additional income would actually be generated if your nonworking spouse got a job? Is it worth it for you to work more overtime? What's the real cost of investing with after-tax dollars? What is a given tax deduction worth? And so on.

Figuring Your Marginal Tax Rate

Your marginal tax rate (or tax bracket) is determined by your *taxable income* and your *filing status*. Taxable income is your gross income less adjustments, exemptions, and deductions (explained later in this chapter). There's a specified income range for each tax rate starting with $0 through $25,350 for single taxpayers and running up to $278,450 and beyond for single taxpayers and others. By law, these income ranges are adjusted each year to account for inflation. (The figures used here and in the table nearby are for 1998.)

There are four filing status designations: Single, Married Filing Jointly, Married Filing Separately, and Head of Household (a single person with dependents). The tax rates are the same in each case. What varies is the income range to which they are applied.

Adjustments, Exemptions, and Deductions

If the tax code stopped there, things would be simple. Unfortunately, it is here that the tax code really *begins*, with its thousands of pages of special deals, conditions, and exceptions. The key thing to remember is that you are taxed not on your gross income but on your *taxable income:* gross income minus adjustments, exemptions, and deductions. The devil may be in the details, but the tax savings are in these various adjustments, exemptions, and deductions:

1998 Tax Rates

Single Taxpayer

Taxable Income	Total Tax	Marginal Tax Rate
Under $25,350	15% of taxable income	15%
$25,350 to $61,400	$3,802 + 28% of amount over $25,350	28%
$61,400 to $128,100	$13,896 + 31% of amount over $61,400	31%
$128,100 to $278,450	$34,573 + 36% of amount over $128,100	36%
Over $278,450	$88,699 + 39.6% of amount over $278,450	39.6%

Married Couple Filing Joint Return

Taxable Income	Total Tax	Marginal Tax Rate
Under $42,350	15% of taxable income	15%
$42,350 to $102,300	$6,352 + 28% of amount over $42,350	28%
$102,300 to 155,950	$23,138 + 31% of amount over $102,300	31%
$155,950 to $278,450	$39,770 + 36% of amount over $155,950	36%
Over $278,450	$83,870 + 39.6% of amount over $278,450	39.6%

Married Couple Filing Separate Returns

Taxable Income	Total Tax	Marginal Tax Rate
Under $21,175	15% of taxable income	15%
$21,175 to $51,150	$3,176 + 28% of amount over $21,175	28%
$51,150 to $77,975	$11,569 + 31% of amount over $51,150	31%
$77,975 to $139,225	$19,885 + 36% of amount over $77,975	36%
Over $139,225	$41,935 + 39.6% of amount over $139,225	39.6%

Head of Household

Taxable Income	Total Tax	Marginal Tax Rate
Under $33,950	15% of taxable income.	15%
$33,950 to $87,700	$5,092 + 28% of amount over $33,950	28%
$87,700 to $142,200	$20,142 +31% of amount over $87,700	31%
$142,200 to $278,450	$36,975 +36% of amount over $142,200	36%
Over $278,450	$86,097 + 39.6% of amount over $278,450	39.6%

• **Adjustments** are amounts you can subtract directly from your gross income for things like contributions to retirement accounts, alimony payments, moving expenses, and self-employment taxes. Your gross income minus any adjustments to which you're entitled gives you your *adjusted gross income* (AGI).

• **Exemptions** allow you to reduce your taxable income by a fixed amount ($2,700 in 1998) for yourself (this is called your *personal exemption*) and for each of your dependents. But once you hit a certain income level, the dollar amount of the exemption is gradually reduced, and it's eliminated entirely at the highest income levels.

• **Deductions** are where the tax code really goes wild. You can choose to take the standard deduction for your filing status—$3,550 to $7,100 in 1998—or you can itemize your deductions. The dollar amount of the standard deduction is higher for those who are sixty-five or older or blind, yet another little twist in the tax code.

You'll learn more about deductions in a moment. But to complete the discussion of the main ways to reduce taxes owed, we must not forget *tax credits*. Tax credits are like money in the bank. That's because you calculate the tax you owe, and then subtract from it any tax credits to which you're entitled. For example, at this writing, the tax code includes a $400-per-child tax credit for families making up to $110,000 a year.

Deductions Are the Key

If you (and your spouse if you're married) work for a salary, and if those salaries are the sole source of your income, the only way to immediately reduce your tax burden is through deductions. The first deductions for you to consider are payroll deductions. Think about how much money you can put into employer-sponsored tax-deferred retirement 401(k) plans. Then consider IRAs and other investment options discussed in chapter 9. You'll still pay taxes on the money, but not until you retire and are presumably in a lower tax bracket. In the meantime, the money compounds and grows tax-free.

Next, compare your standard deduction to a rough estimate of what your total deductions would be if you were to itemize. Itemizing deductions means filling out Schedule A and filing it with your return. Interestingly, according to the IRS, only about 30 percent of taxpayers itemize. To get a quick handle on whether you should go to the trouble, add up the following deductions and compare them to the standard deduction you (or you and your spouse) can take:

• Mortgage interest and points paid on your loan

• State and local income taxes

• Real-estate taxes

• Charitable contributions

If these four items total more than your applicable standard deduction, then you should probably itemize on Schedule A. If these are your only deductions, you can probably prepare and file the return yourself, though you may find it helpful to use a tax-preparation software package like Kiplinger TaxCut or Intuit's TurboTax.

Lots of Other Deductions, but Be Careful!

Once you opt to itemize, many other smaller deductions may be available. These include major medical and dental expenses that exceed some percentage of your AGI (currently 7.5 percent), casualty and theft losses that exceed 10 percent of your AGI, dues to professional organizations, fees to employment agencies, subscriptions to professional journals, and other special expenses.

This sounds inviting, but, frankly, it is here that the typical taxpayer runs into trouble. It isn't always clear what is deductible and what is not, or what percentage of an expense is deductible. But if you hope to fool the Internal Revenue Service by creating fake deductions, forget it.

The IRS has decades of data on tens of millions of taxpayers. Its computers know what most people who earn between $50,000 and $75,000 a year give to charity. If you're in that income range and claim that you gave considerably more than the norm, your form will be kicked out for further review. Or if you live someplace with zip code demographics that are far above what you claim in wages, a red flag will go up.

Cheating on your taxes isn't worth it. And as computers and the software they run become ever more sophisticated, your chances of getting caught rise each year. Even if you have no intention of cheating, if your time has value, the smart, legal, legitimate way to reduce your tax bill to the absolute minimum is to use a tax program or hire a professional.

Use a Program or Hire a Professional

If you're single, pay rent, and have no investment income, you'll probably do fine filing a simple tax form taking the personal exemption and standard deduction. As long as your taxable income is under $50,000, you may file Form 1040EZ. Answer just twelve questions and you're done. If you have income from several sources, want to take IRA deductions and child-care credits, and your taxable income is less than $50,000, you may use Form 1040A. Otherwise, like 70 percent of all taxpayers, you'll use Form 1040.

Do the Math: It Doesn't Make Sense to Do It Yourself!

Anyone who has filled out tax forms using a pencil and pocket calculator groans each year on opening the instruction booklet for Form 1040. "What's New?" the headline chirps, and the "Tip" box advises, "For details on these and other changes, see What's Hot at www.irs.ustreas.gov." Double groan: new treatment of capital-gains distributions, special new exclusions on the sale of your home, adoption expenses, spousal IRAs; then there are medical savings accounts (MSAs), long-term-care insurance, earned income credit changes, and more. These are just a few of the "what's new" changes in the tax law you can expect to confront, and you will need a special IRS publication and possibly a special form to deal with nearly every one of them

Life is too short and your time is too valuable to spend much of it wrestling with the ever-changing complexities of the tax code. If your financial life is simple, file 1040EZ. If it is a bit more complex, use a tax-preparation program. But if you've got investments, stock options, special benefits and perks, unusual expenses, or if you own a business—even a part-time business you operate out of your home—get help. Hire a tax professional. And that does not mean some high-school math teacher who is moonlighting as a temporary tax-form preparer for some national chain.

That may sound like a severe criticism of tax-preparation firms that open and staff temporary offices in January and close them after April 15. It is not. Many of these firms and the individuals who work for them do excellent work. The problem is, who do you call in August when you want advice on the tax consequences of buying or selling a particular investment? Who do you call when you need guidance on the tax and benefit consequences of your spouse going back to work full time?

As noted at the beginning of this chapter, taxes are a fact of adult life. And the tax code is constantly changing. So just as it makes good sense to have a family doctor, it makes good sense to have a family tax specialist. The cost will probably be about $125 to $200.

But think of it this way. Suppose the charge is $200. If you're married and filing jointly, and your taxable income is over $100,000 a year, you're in the 31 percent tax bracket. Since the fees of tax-preparation professionals are fully deductible, your actual cost is $200 less 31 percent, or $138.

Now, if you have to spend the IRS-reported average of about twelve hours preparing your own return, you will be "earning" about $11.50 an hour by doing it yourself. (And don't forget the $15 you'll have to spend on a copy of the current J. K. Lasser's or some other tax-preparation guide.) And probably you'll either make a mistake or miss some deduction or some more advantageous way of treating a deduction—after all, keeping up to date on the intricacies of the tax code is not your profession.

Tax-Professional Options

You might consider using an *enrolled agent*, a person accredited by the IRS and certified by the Treasury Department, who can represent you before the IRS in an audit or an appeal. (This is something the employees of most storefront, temporary tax-preparation services cannot do.) Fees are usually in the $100-to-$300 range. You'll find them in your local phone directory's yellow pages under "Tax Return Preparation Services" or some such.

However, if you are a professional, a corporate executive, a business owner, or someone who has a similarly complex financial life, you should probably hire a *Certified Public Accountant* (CPA). A CPA will typically prepare your return, advise you on all financial matters, and represent you in the event of an IRS audit. As licensed professionals, CPAs aren't going to jeopardize their jobs by suggesting that you do anything questionable or illegal. But the good ones live and breathe tax law

STREET SMARTS

Twenty-eight-year-old Amy prides herself on doing her own taxes every year. "I usually start by calling the IRS toll-free number. It's easy to remember—800-TAX-FORM. As for the forms themselves, you can order anything you want from the IRS, of course. But it's faster and more convenient to get them from the Internet or America Online."

There's one twist to obtaining tax forms online. You'll need a special program to view and print them: Adobe Acrobat Reader. The program is available at all tax form sites:

IRS Publications and Forms
800-TAX-FORM
www.irs.ustreas.gov

1040.com
www.1040.com

America Online (AOL)
Keyword: Tax forms

and thus know how to handle things so that you pay the lowest tax. CPAs charge by the hour, and typical tax-preparation fees are in the $500-to-$2,500 range.

Charges for advice are discretionary. If you have a relationship with a CPA, you can usually call for answers to quick questions at no charge. Questions that require more time and analysis will probably incur a charge of some sort.

The main event, however, is your tax return, and here the amount you will be charged will be based on the time the person has to spend sifting through your records and preparing your return. This is one instance where your personal computer practically can pay for itself in a single transaction. If you use a personal-finance program like Microsoft Money, Quicken, or Managing Your Money throughout the year, you can probably assemble most of the necessary tax records in a couple of hours. This will greatly reduce the time your tax person will have to spend sorting through the typical "shoebox" of canceled checks and receipts that most people bring in. (See chapter 1 for more information on personal-finance software.)

Extensions

It's become a standard feature of the evening news programs on April 15: stories and film footage showing anxious taxpayers lining up at the post office to file their tax returns before the midnight filing deadline. Most people don't know it, but everyone is entitled to an automatic four-month extension to August 15, no questions

The Fool's Approach

David and Tom Gardner, hosts of the popular Motley Fool investment site on the Internet and America Online, offer some excellent advice on how to find and select a tax accountant or tax preparer. It's a five-step program:

1. Ask around. Talk to others in your profession or business about the people they've used and whether they've been satisfied.

2. Try to find someone who knows your business. Tax law is complex, so you don't want to hire someone who knows the service business if your business is manufacturing.

3. Pay candidates a visit. Any worthy candidate should be willing to give you an hour to discuss your situation, needs, and desires. This will give you a chance to get a sense of the person and the firm and what they will do for you as a client. And don't be shy about asking how fees are set.

4. The more questions the accountant asks *you*, the better. Asking questions shows interest, of course, but questions can also reflect selectivity borne of success and skill.

Someone who asks a lot of questions probably doesn't plan to take every client who walks in the door.

5. Don't overlook the personal: Find someone you're comfortable with. Though not as personal as the doctor/patient relationship, the relationship you have with your accountant is likely to be far more personal than the one you have with your lawyer. To do their jobs effectively, accountants need to know absolutely everything about your financial life. And you need to feel free to call on your accountant for advice throughout the year.

For more "Foolish" wisdom, visit the Motley Fool site on the Internet (www.fool.com) or on America Online (Keyword: Fool).

THE BOTTOM LINE

Taxes are a fact of life. And they aren't all bad. What's bad is the current federal tax code, riddled as it is with all kinds of special conditions and exceptions. But the tax code, too, is a fact of life. The chances of it being swept away and replaced with a clean, simple, fair tax system are highly unlikely. Too many interests benefit from keeping things just the way they are. That is reality.

Unless yours is a very simple financial life, get yourself a tax-preparation software package that is "smart enough" to know about the current tax law, or hire a tax professional. You don't expect to be your own doctor or your own lawyer, so why would you try to serve as your own tax professional? After all, medicine and the law are child's play compared to the federal tax code!

asked. Just file Form 4868. An additional extension beyond August 15 is also possible, if you have a good reason. Use Form 2688 to apply for that.

The one caveat is that any extensions you are granted are for *filing* your tax form, not for paying the taxes due. So it's important to make sure that you've correctly estimated your tax liability for the year and paid at least that amount, or very close to it. Extensions give you time to get your records in order and to prepare your return. They do not give you more time to pay what you owe.

If you're self-employed and contribute to a Keogh or Simplified Employee Pension Plan (SEP), you'll have until the due date of your return, including extensions, to make contributions to the plan.

Wills, Trusts, and Estate Planning

This is a book about money—how to get it, how to keep it, how to make it grow, and how to use it to protect your life, health, and family. And, of course, how to legally shield as much of it as you can from taxes. You've worked hard. You've paid attention. Now you have a nice nest egg to pass along to help your kids and your grandchildren—whether they want to buy a home, go to college, start a business, or whatever.

But just as you are slipping into your last sleep and "going into the Light," you hear someone say, "Don't go yet. If you don't sign these papers, the government will take everything!"

Well, not everything. It may be as little as 37 percent, but it could be as high as 55 percent. Whatever the percentage, it doesn't make sense. After all, you're dead. So you won't be consuming any goods or government services. Inheritance taxes (or "death taxes" as they're often called) represent a windfall for the government. They aren't fair. They aren't just. After all, it isn't as though the deceased didn't pay all kinds of other taxes throughout his or her life. But they are the law. Take that as a given.

Estate-Planning Goals

Fortunately, there are other laws that can protect you, laws that have virtually no impact on how you live but a huge impact on the disposition of your wealth when you die. And not to oversimplify, but it all comes down to whether or not you've signed a few papers. As always, procrastination is your greatest enemy. So let's get started!

There are three main goals in estate planning:

• Ensuring that your property is distributed according to your wishes.

• Avoiding or minimizing delays caused by the process of probating the will.

• Minimizing the taxes collected from your estate.

Start with Your Will

If you don't have a will, you've got a lot of company. *Consumer Reports* says that nearly 70 percent of American adults don't have wills. It's understandable. After all, no one likes to think about leaving this earth. But if you care for your heirs, you will take the time and spend the money needed to prepare a will.

You'll have to name an executor to manage the distribution of your property after you're gone. If you have young children, you'll have to name a guardian. And the more specific you are in detailing who gets what, the better.

If your affairs are simple, you might want to take a first crack at things with a program you can run on your personal computer. One of the most popular and highly rated is Nolo Press's Willmaker software, available for $42 when you buy it directly from Nolo. Hiring a lawyer, on the other hand, will cost between $500 and $1,000. But you may well decide it's worth it to take that route, because each state has different, even quirky, laws about wills and inheritances.

For example, wills must usually be witnessed

F.Y.I.

In New York and New Jersey, probating a will takes several months and typically costs between $200 and $1,000. In California, however, the process can take up to two years and cost 6 percent or more of the assets in the estate.

by three people. But in some states, a witness cannot be a beneficiary. So if you plan to leave anything to your daughter, do *not* have her as one of your official witnesses! Also, in some states, if you leave someone a property with a mortgage, the estate might be forced to pay off the mortgage unless you include language in your will specifically stating otherwise.

Avoiding Probate

Probate courts were created originally to "prove" a will to be valid or invalid—and, not incidentally, to make sure the state gets its share of your assets. (New York uses the term Surrogate's Court. In Pennsylvania, it's called Orphan's Court.) But over the years, the role of probate courts has expanded to include oversight and administration of wills. Probate courts make sure that your assets are protected against theft or loss once you're no longer here. And they make sure your bills and taxes are paid.

Probate courts perform another very important function as well—making sure that your assets go to your beneficiaries as specified in your will. That doesn't sound like much, but without the court's decree stating who succeeds to the ownership of the property, title to the property would remain in the name of the deceased. That means the property could not be sold or transferred because a potential purchaser would have no way of determining who owns it and can thus legally sell it. The probate court's judicial decree resolves this uncertainty.

In most cases, the person you have appointed

as executor will be responsible for doing the actual work of consolidating your assets, notifying your creditors, paying your taxes, and so on. But the court must review the details, and this can take time, often months and sometimes years.

Fortunately, there are three main ways to avoid having your estate be put through probate:

1. Naming a beneficiary for each specific asset you own (bank account, securities account, life insurance policy, retirement account, among others).

2. Putting your property into joint tenancy (ownership) with right of survivorship.

3. Putting all your assets into a revocable trust.

Named Beneficiaries

Writing in the *CPA Journal,* attorney and adjunct professor Timothy P. O'Sullivan explains why naming beneficiaries for each of your assets helps to keep them out of probate:

Beneficiary designations under life insurance policies, retirement plans—e.g., pension, profit sharing, and 401(k)s—and IRAs avoid probate because they constitute contractual or trust obligations specifying the persons to whom proceeds should be paid. For example, under a life insurance policy, a policy owner contracts with the life insurance company to pay out a death benefit to a designated beneficiary or beneficiaries. There is no need for a probate court decree specifying who should receive

SMART MONEY

"In recent years," writes Jane Bryant Quinn, syndicated financial columnist for *Newsweek,* "many states have passed probate-simplification laws, especially for small estates or estates in which everything passes to the spouse. There may also be speedy procedures for estates that aren't contested."

The simplified procedures are known as the Uniform Probate Code. The Code was first published by the National Conference of Commissioners on Uniform State Laws in 1969. Your attorney or the clerk of your county's probate court should be able to tell you more about it.

the insurance proceeds because that has already been provided by contract.

Naturally, there are twists and turns. In states lacking "payable on death" beneficiary provisions, financial accounts that are not jointly owned or owned by a trust must go through probate. And in general, real estate cannot be designated to a beneficiary in order to avoid probate.

You'll also want to bear in mind that by designating a specific beneficiary for each of your assets, you may inadvertently give more to one person than another, when an even division was your intent.

The Joint Tenancy (Ownership) Option

Bearing in mind that one of the main functions of a probate court is to establish clear title to the property of the deceased, if you and a friend, relative, or spouse own a property jointly and you die, there is usually no question about who owns the property. Succession is automatic, so there is no need for a probate court's determination.

There are just two main potential stumbling blocks. First, retirement plans and IRAs can't be owned jointly. Second, for properties that are jointly owned, you must be sure to specify "with right of survivorship" on the deed, title, or other ownership document. Your lawyer can tell you more, but basically, you must make it clear that you and your joint tenant desire the property to pass to whomever survives the other.

The downside to joint tenancy is that a person

named as a joint tenant becomes a co-owner. While you're still alive, he or she could quite legally take the asset, cash it in, and run away with the money.

The Living Trust Option

A trust is a legal entity, rather like a corporation, that can own, buy, sell, or transfer property. And, just as a corporation is managed by its officers, a trust is managed by one or more trustees. There are many kinds of trusts, but for the sake of argument, assume you create a trust, name yourself as the trustee, and transfer all of your assets into that trust. Technically, you will no longer own the assets. But you can control them just as you did before. And your death has no real impact on the disposition of the trust's assets, since it didn't die, one of its trustees (you) did.

Since you own no assets when you die, there is no need to go through probate. When you die, the named trustee (or successor trustee) has authority to pay your bills and has a fiduciary responsibility to distribute the trust properly to beneficiaries as provided in the provisions of the trust. A trust is the only device that can be used with all types of property and does not depend upon the survival of specific persons to avoid probate.

A *living trust* (also known as a *revocable trust* or *inter vivos revocable trust*), can be altered or changed by you as you see fit. It is in many respects a paper transaction: You give all of your assets to the trust but you make yourself the trustee, so you continue to use them just as you did before. (Technically, an *irrevocable trust* requires you to permanently give up control of

STREET SMARTS

"Moving a life insurance policy into a trust can be a really easy way to transfer wealth free of estate taxes," advises Eleanor, a tax attorney with a large Los Angeles firm. "You'll want to talk to your own tax adviser about your situation. There are several options: You can have a trust buy the policy in the first place, so you are never the owner. If you already have a policy, you can put it into an irrevocable trust. The main twist here is that you've got to live at least three years after the transfer into the trust or your estate will be taxed anyway. Also, if it's a cash-value policy and the current value is greater than the $10,000-a-year exclusion, the transfer may be subject to gift tax."

the assets you transfer to it, but in reality the conditions of the trust can give you considerable control over how its assets are used.)

Living Trusts: Advantages

Living trusts are not for everyone. And they are far from the only "trustlike" option. You should also know that stories abound of unscrupulous salespeople who zero in on retirement communities to sell living trusts to elderly residents. Typically there will be a free seminar, during which the speakers will grossly exaggerate the costs of probating a will. Then a salesperson will call and present a sales pitch offering to set up a living trust for $2,000 or more.

The salespeople are rarely legally qualified to sell such services, their services are usually vastly overpriced, and the trust documents they prepare often do not pass legal muster. Talk to your lawyer. Talk to your accountant or tax preparer. Don't let yourself be taken.

That said, legitimate living trusts have some advantages over wills:

• **They are not public records.** As a public document, anyone who is interested can get a copy of your will and the disposition of your assets. This doesn't happen with living trusts.

• **Possible cost savings.** The assets owned by a living trust are not subject to probate costs and additional attorney fees that would be incurred in a probate estate. If you own property in two or more states, this can be a major factor, because without a living trust, your will would have to be probated in each of those states.

• **Coordination of your estate plan.** A living trust coordinates your entire estate plan and all assets through a single instrument. That can help you avoid the problem of inadvertently leaving property to beneficiaries in disproportionate amounts, as might happen with the joint tenancy or beneficiary designations discussed earlier.

• **Stability.** Normally, revocable trusts do not need to be changed when you move to another state.

Living Trusts: Disadvantages

Naturally, there are potential disadvantages of going with a living trust instead of a will, including the following:

• **Greater initial expense and effort.** You can expect to pay between $1,500 and $3,000 to have an attorney create a living trust. (It all depends on the complexity of your estate.)

• **Forgetting to put all assets into the trust.** A living trust is useless if you do not immediately transfer all of your assets into it. (You'll probably need a lawyer's help with this.) But what if you acquire a property and forget to transfer it to the trust? Sorry. Welcome to probate court for that asset.

• **The legal legwork involved.** You can't wave a wand and automatically transfer all of your assets to a living trust. Deeds have to be changed, documents have to be filed, and paperwork must be done. You will have to pay someone (your lawyer) to do this.

Minimizing Taxes on Your Estate

Living trusts do *not* save taxes. They are a vehicle for avoiding probate costs and delays and nothing more. If a salesperson or someone else has told you something else, you should question that person's expertise at the very least.

Still, minimizing the tax bite is one of the main goals of estate planning. So, by way of background, you need to know that in 1998, you can transfer $625,000 to your heirs tax-free. The allowable amount rises by about $25,000 a year until the year 2006, when it reaches one million dollars. The value of your estate above the current exemption will be taxed by the federal government at 37 to 55 percent. And additional state death taxes may also apply.

So how can you minimize the chunk of your estate that goes for taxes? There are lots of techniques, but few of them are simple, and none of them can be reliably used without a good attorney or accountant.

• **Bypass trusts.** If you're married and you die, you can pass along up to $625,000 to your spouse tax-free (in 1998). But when your spouse dies, that money will be part of his or her estate. That's why it is often better to will the money to a bypass trust (earmarked, say, for your kids) that lets your surviving spouse collect income from it and possibly even use the principal. Because the money is held by the trust, it's not considered part of the surviving spouse's estate when he or she dies and thus is not subject to tax. (But make sure your attorney

Durable Power of Attorney

When you grant someone *power of attorney*, you're giving that person the right to pay your bills and otherwise manage your financial affairs when you're not able to do so yourself. There are variations to cover most situations—such as if you are going to be out of the country for several months and need someone to pay your bills—but the real danger is if you become mentally disabled, at which point the typical power-of-attorney document expires.

To protect yourself in that situation, you need to have your attorney draw up a *durable* power of attorney. (The forms offered for sale at many office-supply stores may also be perfectly adequate.) This lets someone act on your behalf if you are judged senile or mentally disabled, if you fall into a coma, or if you are otherwise unable to make your own decisions. Once you recover, you can revoke a durable power of attorney at your convenience. There are many variations and details, so, as always, consult your attorney.

One crucial point: Your bank, broker, and insurance company may want you to fill out their forms before agreeing to your durable-power-of-attorney request.

includes provisions necessary to account for the rising federal death tax "exemption" instead of specifying a given dollar amount.)

• **Qualified personal-residence trusts.** Here's an example from *SmartMoney Interactive* (on the Web at www.smartmoney.com): A seventy-four-year-old retired doctor wants to give his Florida beachfront home (estimated value: $1 million) to his two daughters, removing it from his estate and thus from the taxman's reach. So, in consultation with his attorney, he puts the home in an irrevocable trust for seven years:

Through a complex IRS calculation based on interest rates, the length of the

THE BOTTOM LINE

Your signature on the right piece of paper can make a difference of tens of thousands of dollars in what your kids and grandkids inherit. So take the time to find the right attorney, one who specializes in trusts and estates, to handle things for you.

Treat this chapter as a wake-up call. Spend some money and get some really good professional advice about how to structure your estate. After all, what's the point of working hard all your life only to have the federal and state governments take a huge bite out of your assets when you die, simply because you didn't take the time or spend the money to plan and because you neglected to sign a few papers?

trust, and his age, the IRS values his right to live in the house at $625,000. For the purposes of his estate, that knocks the value of his house down to $375,000—regardless of how much the house appreciates in the meantime. When the trust is up, if he chooses to continue living there, he can pay his daughters rent, further reducing the size of his estate.

As always, there are risks. The doctor's kids could legally throw him out on the street since they now own the property. And should the doctor die before the trust expires, the house reverts to his estate and no tax benefits accrue. Still, this is a good example of how a few changes on paper that will not affect your life have the potential to save a great deal in taxes when you die.

• **The unified credit: Give it away now!** You can give anyone $10,000 a year tax-free. And so can your spouse, even if he or she does not earn an income. There are recapture provisions on your death, and the recipient may owe tax on the money (but at a lower rate than your estate would pay). The main idea is to get the money out of your estate. There are ways to make sure that it is used for specific purposes—like a grandchild's college education and not the hot new car he or she may crave. Once again, see your attorney for details.

Index